Data Protection and the New UK GDPR Landscape

Author
Frank Suttie

Managing director
Sian O'Neill

Data Protection and the New UK GDPR Landscape
is published by

Globe Law and Business Ltd
3 Mylor Close
Horsell
Woking
Surrey GU21 4DD
United Kingdom
Tel: +44 20 3745 4770
www.globelawandbusiness.com

Printed and bound in Great Britain by Ashford Colour Press Ltd

Data Protection and the New UK GDPR Landscape

ISBN 9781787423701
EPUB ISBN 9781787423718
Adobe PDF ISBN 9781787423725
Mobi ISBN 9781787423732

Table of contents

Introduction

Why publish a Special Report on data protection laws in the UK?

The answer is simple. Data protection law has undoubtedly become one of the most important areas of our legal system due to the vast advances in technology that have taken place over some three decades now, which in turn have led to the collation and processing of huge amounts of data.

It is also a particularly controversial area of our legal system, with privacy interest groups pitted against innovators and entrepreneurs, all working tirelessly with privacy campaigners seemingly responding to every new technological development with demands for ever-greater controls over data.

It is this background that has shaped our privacy laws. We saw by far the greatest step change in our data protection legislation in May 2018 with the coming into effect of Regulation (EU) 2016/679 of the European Parliament and of the Council of 27 April 2016 on the protection of natural persons with regard to the processing of personal data and on the free movement of such data – a piece of legislation better known as the General Data Protection Regulation or GDPR. This reworking and further development of the law relating to the privacy of the individual proved so significant that the acronym

GDPR instantly entered our vocabulary – and, as we shall see, remains in our vocabulary even after the exit of the UK from the EU.

The GDPR has presented business owners, management teams, public authorities and even the smallest of charities with significant new compliance obligations. Many of those affected struggle to put in place internal resources to ensure that they meet the compliance requirements; they have therefore recourse – more than they perhaps wish to – to professional advisers to draft privacy notices and advise them on data breaches. The call upon the time of professional advisers in May 2018 was significant, with many of them tested on their own understanding of an area of law that is, for many, easy neither to assimilate nor to relate to in a way that leads to sound legal advice.

This Special Report is intended to support the process of giving that sound advice. Focus is on the key deliverables expected of an adviser – understanding just what personal data is (not as straightforward as it may sound), how to draft effective and compliant privacy notices and how to respond to the expectations of data subjects when rights afforded to individuals are exercised.

The report covers many other topics, some in areas that businesses and others affected struggle with, in the author's experience. To give one example: the particularly onerous process that a data controller should undertake when entrusting another party with personal data for processing.

To maintain the readability of this Special Report and in recognition that this is not a textbook, a number of subjects are covered only briefly. With this in mind, tribute can be paid to the Information Commissioner's Office (ICO) which, as part of its responsibilities, has worked hard to further develop the data protection landscape not just through guidance and enforcement, but also through education. Some of the references quoted in this report will take the reader to the ICO's online resources. These are presented in a particularly effective way, providing self-assessment questions around compliance and steering the reader towards even deeper understanding of the compliance expectations that the ICO has.

This Special Report was completed in early January 2021, just as the EU-UK Trade and Cooperation Agreement entered into provisional effect as a treaty between EU member states and the UK. While it was hoped that issues relating to the continued transfer of personal data between EU member states (and also those comprising the European Economic Area (EEA)) would be addressed within the same timescale through an EU 'adequacy' decision,[1] this outcome has not been achieved. An interim period has been agreed[2] during which personal data may continue to be passed from the EEA to the UK for processing pending the conclusion of deliberations within the EU concerning whether the UK privacy laws meet the standards required for an adequacy decision.

This Special Report reflects the way data protection legislation will apply in the UK now that the country has left the EU. An EU adequacy decision in relation to the UK data protection legislation is expected to be taken and, as is explained in this publication, a grace period of up to six months has been provided for. Should an EU adequacy decision not be achieved, the procedures referred to in this report concerning international transfers to third countries will be relevant to the processing of personal data within the UK of data originating from the EU.

I. A brief history of data protection in the UK

1. Introduction

Concern over the privacy of individuals has existed for longer than might be thought. Even before the emergence of computers, activists were lobbying for personal privacy. Evidence exists for example[3] in the form of a treatise – The Right to Privacy – in which the authors (US lawyers Samuel D Warren and Louis D Brandeis) promoted the concept of privacy as being "a right to be left alone".

Jump forward to 1948 and the legacy of the Second World War begins to influence matters of privacy with the adoption of the Universal Declaration of Human Rights.

The emergence of affordable information technology in the 1970s then led to an exponential growth in the collection and storage of data – including personal data. Slowly but surely, momentum in the promotion of personal privacy and the protection of personal data began to rise as a socially significant issue, rapidly becoming a challenge presented by society to governments across the world.

In 1980 the Organisation for Economic Co-Operation and Development became one of the first global organisations to appreciate and address the significance of the need to take measures to protect personal data in order to counter-balance the fast-increasing opportunities to exploit data collected from, or relating to, individuals.

A year later the Council of Europe adopted the Data Protection Convention.[4] This treaty effectively marked the beginning of the period in which European countries started to address just exactly what legislative measures should be adopted at national level. In many ways, Europe has led the way in the development of data protection legislation.

At a national level, it is arguably the UK that led the way in creating a legal regime of personal data protection with the enactment of the Data Protection Act 1984. That statute set out a basic framework of compliance requirements at a time when the internet was still, in relative terms, in its infancy and the capability to store data was limited.

The 1984 act introduced a series of principles to be followed when personal data was being processed, created a number of offences associated with compliance duties and introduced a requirement to register with the then Office of the Data Protection Registrar. Perhaps most importantly, the act introduced the principle of compensation for individuals whose personal data had been compromised.

By far the most significant milestone, though, has been the coordinated efforts of the member states of the European Community (as it then was) leading to the adoption of Directive 95/46/EC of the European Parliament and of the Council of 24 October 1995 on the protection of individuals with regard to the processing of personal data (the European Data Protection Directive). Key concepts that came into existence at that time, and which have played a major role in the continuing development of data protection, included the concept of the individual's consent being required for the processing of personal data and the development of the scope of protection through the definition of the scope of processing activities. It even introduced, at this relatively early stage, a concept that some data processed concerning an individual would carry with it particular sensitivities.

To create a collaborative network of regulators across the EU, Article 29 of the European Data Protection Directive provided for the creation of a committee which became known as the Article 29 Working Party. The aim of the working party was to provide expert advice to member states, secure as much consistency as possible in relation to the application of the directive and fulfil various other advisory tasks – including through the publication of guidance material. Under the GDPR, the working party has become the European Data Protection Board.

The UK adopted the 1995 directive through the enactment of the Data Protection Act 1998, which repealed the Data Protection Act 1984. The outcome was legislation that provided greater protection for personal data linked to the harmonisation of rules relating to the collecting, retaining and processing of personal data across EU member states.

The European Data Protection Directive, however, soon proved to have limited impact on the rapidly expanding practices of electronic marketing which had emerged over the 1990s thanks to greater access to technology. E-marketing became a significant issue in itself and, consequently, in need of specific legislative attention.

In the UK, this took the form of the Privacy and Electronic Communications Regulations 2003. The regulations focus on electronic communications in their various forms. Specific rules capture activities including:

- cookies placed on computers and other electronic devices;
- marketing telephone calls, texts and facsimiles;
- maintaining security of data within communication services; and
- customer privacy in a number of functional areas including GPS data, itemised billing systems, line identification and even directory listings.

"The European Data Protection Directive soon proved to have limited impact on the rapidly expanding practices of electronic marketing which had emerged over the 1990s."

The year 2010 marked the next milestone, with the framework for privacy by design published the previous year gaining international acceptance when the International Assembly of Privacy Commissioners and Data Protection Authorities unanimously passed a resolution recognising the framework (and underlying methodology) as an international standard. Among other commitments, the privacy commissioners resolved to promote privacy by design as widely as possible and foster the incorporation of the principle into policy and legislation.

Meanwhile, advances in information technology continued apace, notably with access to technology through increasingly powerful devices, such as mobile phones transforming into smartphones and, more recently, the internet of things bringing digital communication into other commonplace domestic items.

The most recent review of EU data protection laws began in January 2012 with the publication by the European Commission of a proposal for legislation to reform data protection and, interestingly, with the intent of strengthening the EU digital economy. The European Commission was effectively saying that failure to grasp the nettle in terms of updating essential data protection laws would hold back the digital economy – with individuals deterred from engaging in digital

"From an early stage in the Brexit negotiations, the UK made it clear that it was willing to agree that once the UK became a 'third country', its successor legal regime would be sufficiently robust to be regarded as providing adequate protection for EU citizens' personal data."

transactions cross-border due to uncertainties concerning their personal data protection rights.

With this issue under consideration, it is then no surprise that the EU decided to take a different tool from its kit and make the basis of data protection reform not a directive (involving local implementation at member state level), but a regulation directly enforceable in member states once in force.

The proposed legislation received strong support through its legislative process, notably in the European Parliament where the regulation attracted 621 votes for (with only 10 against and 21 abstentions). Common agreement by all EU institutions involved in the process was achieved on 15 December 2015.

And so, 27 April 2016 saw the passage into law of what is now known as the GDPR, with the coming into effect of the legislation set for 25 May 2018. In compliance with its duties as an EU member state, the UK had to start enforcing the GDPR directly from that date, which it has done effectively; as will be seen in section 2 below, the UK also enacted domestic legislation to complement the GDPR.

However, the period between the enactment of the GDPR and its coming into force saw the Brexit referendum take place, leading to negotiations for the withdrawal of the UK from the EU. The UK's exit from the EU at 11pm on 31 December 2020 followed a period (known as the 'transitional period') during which the UK agreed to continue to observe EU law and be subject to its institutions.

From an early stage in the Brexit negotiations, the UK made it clear that it was willing to agree that once the UK became a 'third country', its successor legal regime would be sufficiently robust to be regarded as providing adequate protection for EU citizens' personal data (a key requirement for effective personal data exchanges under the GDPR). Accordingly, a statutory instrument[5] (subsequently amended) was adopted under the European Union (Withdrawal) Act 2018, essentially creating an adapted version of the GDPR and representing the continued acceptance of the principles of EU data protection legislation.

For the purpose of this Special Report, a distinction needs to be made between the EU-adopted GDPR and the UK version. Accordingly, the remainder of this report refers either to the EU GDPR (where it is intended to refer to the GDPR as implemented by the EU) or the UK GDPR (where referring to the UK adapted version). For ease of reading, most references to the UK GDPR are simplified to just GDPR. While many consequential amendments have been required to allow the UK GDPR to operate effectively, it is notable that article reference numbers from the EU GDPR have been fully preserved.

2. What is the purpose of the Data Protection Act 2018?

The decision by the UK government to promote primary legislation, notwithstanding the direct implementation of the EU GDPR into UK law, is for the following reasons:

- The EU is not comprehensively competent to legislate in relation to all matters that it is expected data protection legislation should affect. Part 2 of the Data Protection Act 2018 provides additional data protection legislation specific to the UK – for example, confirming the child consent threshold age at 13 and an appropriate definitional scope for a public authority, these being subject to the GDPR in particular ways.
- The EU determined not to provide directly applicable data protection provisions associated with law enforcement or security surveillance in the EU GDPR. The former was addressed through an EU directive[6] (referred to below as the Law Enforcement Directive), while the latter fell outside of EU competence. Parts 3 and 4 of the Data Protection Act 2018 addressed these requirements respectively.

It is important to appreciate not just the scope of the GDPR, but also what is not addressed within that scope. Table 1 provides a useful summary, which in turn also explains the role played by the Data Protection Act 2018 and other less familiar legislation.

3. Key points of emphasis under the EU GDPR

The implementation of the EU GDPR marked a major step change in the recognition of personal privacy. The further responsibilities added to data controllers were significant – most notably, in terms of having the greatest effect, the need to revisit and redraw privacy notices to align with the requirements of the EU GDPR and to take, in a formal way, much more responsibility around decisions to appoint processors to handle personal data on behalf of the data controller.

The compliance burden affected all corners of our society, with responsibilities placed not just on businesses but also individuals engaged in business activities, charities and other third-sector organisations. Unincorporated bodies such as clubs and societies, no matter how small, are affected as, indeed, they were under previous data protection legislation.

The EU GDPR seeks to address a number of risks to the security of personal data. Principles that will be explained in this respect include:

- the principle of accountability;
- the introduction of data protection officers (DPOs);
- the protection of children;
- a more granular approach to securing consent permitting data processing;
- responsibilities of a data processor emphasised;
- profiling;
- protection for special category data; and
- formalisation of the requirement for data protection impact assessments.

4. The first two years of the EU GDPR

The European Commission is required to monitor progress in the implementation of the EU GDPR and published its first report in June 2020.[7] The report notes the role that the commission has in

Table 1. The role of the Data Protection Act 2018 and other legislation

Timeline	EU		UK				
	EU GDPR (2016/679)	EU Law Enforcement Directive (2016/680)	Data Protection Act 2018				UK GDPR
			Part 1	Part 2	Part 3	Part 4	
Pre-Brexit	Applicable	Applicable, implemented into UK law by Parts 3 and 4 of the Data Protection Act 2018	Introductory provisions	Supplemental provisions modifying the scope of the EU GDPR in relation to activities outside of the competence of the EU. Schedule 6 provides detailed scope	Law Enforcement Data Processing implementing EU Law Enforcement Directive (2016/680)	Intelligence Services Data Processing	Not applicable
Post-Brexit	Not applicable	Not applicable	Continues to apply	Continues to apply	Continues to apply	Continues to apply	Applicable

monitoring national implementation within member states and, in doing this, highlights some fragmentation arising from the flexibilities that have been provided within the GDPR. Differences in defining the age limit for an individual to be treated as a child is cited as one example.

Empowering individuals to control their own personal data is very much an aspiration within the data protection regime. The requirement for data portability – discussed in Chapter XI – is noted as an area in which much more progress is regarded as achievable.

5. The GDPR post-Brexit

With effect from 11pm on 31 December 2020, the EU regards the UK as a 'third country', meaning that unless an adequacy decision is taken, as explained in Chapter XIV, organisations based in the EU will be required to take extra steps to maintain data sharing and data processing activities that involve UK businesses but where the personal data is that of EU subjects.

This exercise is a significant one, particularly for small and medium-sized enterprises, and involves developing and implementing quite complex legal documentation.[8]

A pragmatic position is adopted in the EU-UK Trade and Cooperation Agreement. This provides what may be described as a 'grace period' of up to four months (extendable to six months without any requirement for notice from either party) to enable a determination relating to adequacy of the UK data protection regime to be made under Article 44 of the EU GDPR.

To go back to the purpose of this Special Report mentioned in the introduction – namely, to support the process of giving sound advice in relation to the GDPR requirements by focusing on the key deliverables expected of an adviser – let us now consider in detail what personal data is, how to draft effective and compliant privacy notices and how to respond to the expectations of data subjects when rights afforded to individuals are exercised – among other aspects.

II. Personal data, control and processing defined

1. What counts as 'personal data' and who are controllers and processors?

The scope of data protection legislation is living individuals.
A deceased person no longer satisfies the criteria for protection.

To determine whether data held counts as 'personal data' involves the following initial considerations:

- Can the individual the data relates to be identified directly from the information that has been provided or which the individual has agreed can be sourced from a third party?
- Can the person be indirectly identified from that information in combination with other information that the potential data controller is able to access without the specific agreement of the individual?

'Personal data' has its definition in Article 4(1) of the GDPR, which provides the following non-exhaustive list: name, identification number, location data, online identifier or one or more factors specific to the physical, physiological, genetic, mental, economic, cultural or social identity of that natural person.

A key test is whether the element of data at issue relates to the individual. The best comparison is to consider the data associated with a specific person. A procurement manager within an organisation may be responsible for sourcing supplies of various products. If you are a supplier to that business, the information you hold regarding the goods ordered by that individual will certainly not be personal data. The mobile telephone number you hold as a point of contact with that individual may well be for a mobile used for personal purposes by that person and should therefore be assumed to be personal data.

Case study

Why are IP addresses 'personal data'?

A consumer browses the online catalogue of a fashion retailer. As soon as she commences browsing, she is asked to accept cookies (tiny data items placed on the user's device) – which she does. As she carries on browsing, data associated with exactly what she reviews on the site is being captured. She is not ready to make a purchase yet. The retailer therefore knows there has been browsing activity from a particular location but has no information yet as to the identity of the browser.

A few days later, the same consumer comes back to the site and makes a purchase of a single item. The retailer now has the ability to match the browsing activity to the individual as it now has access to other, more meaningful personal data of the individual. And since a purchase has been made, marketing activity can now start with a carefully crafted message directed to that consumer reminding her about what else she took a look at.

2. Data controllers – when is an organisation characterised as a 'data controller'?

Labelling in data protection law is always focused on the function involved. The ability to make decisions concerning the processing of personal data is the key determining factor. Notably, a data controller may of course be concerned with the processing of the data, but where the data controller involves other parties in the processing, attention needs to turn to the status of the processor: if the transferee receives instructions to process the data in particular ways, it will be acting as a data processor for that data. If, however, the data is passed to that other party with the intention that the transferee takes advantage of the data for purposes of its own, then the relationship is one termed 'data sharing'.

An example of the latter situation arises when an NHS hospital trust is required to pass personal data to commissioning groups which will take that personal data and use it for their purposes – these purposes being very likely different to the purposes for which the personal data was originally collected.

The fact that the trust stores data does not in itself make the trust the data controller for that data – it is necessary to look at matters in more detail.

Starting with the data controller role, it is crucial for an organisation to understand if it holds that status. As we shall see in Chapter V, being a data controller places a range of responsibilities on the organisation that a data processor does not have.

Article 4(7) of the GDPR defines 'data controller' as:

> *the natural or legal person, public authority, agency or other body which, alone or jointly with others, determines the purposes and means of the processing of Personal Data.*

It is clear from this that the test is twofold – namely:

- a purposive test – personal data is held for a reason and the motivations of the organisation concerned need to be considered along with the fact that the organisation actively uses the data in particular ways in its own interests; and
- a functional test – the organisation determines what processing

"Being a data controller places a range of responsibilities on the organisation that a data processor does not have."

of the data takes place (eg, applying an algorithm to the personal data creating new personal data as an outcome of the processing).

3. The concept of a joint controller

It is possible for personal data to be under the control of two separate legal entities, each of which will be regarded as having controller responsibilities. Under Article 26 of the GDPR, the criteria to be applied in establishing whether there are circumstances of joint control are as follows:

- there are two or more entities subject to regulation concerned with the personal data; and
- together, through relationships they hold with each other, they can determine the purposes and means of processing.

4. Joint controller – who has the responsibility for compliance?

The concept of joint controller necessarily leads to questions as to who carries the burden of some important responsibilities under data protection laws. By way of example:

- To whom should a data subject access request be addressed?
- Who takes responsibility for the management of data processing that is subcontracted?
- How should information concerning joint control be expressed in privacy notices?

Joint controllers are required to determine the allocation of responsibilities between themselves,[9] but must not attempt to vary their respective legal responsibilities. Data subjects are entitled to exercise rights against all parties acting as joint controllers.

5. Data processors – how is an organisation characterised as a 'data processor'?

It is crucial here to understand the scope of the term 'processing'.

'Processing' is defined in the GDPR as involving operations performed on the data. Article 4(2) provides a long list of activities such as the recording, organisation, alteration and retrieval of the personal data.

Essentially, anything that happens to the data is likely to constitute processing. Even holding data at rest – sitting as a record in a database or stored in a library of hard copy documents – is considered processing of the data concerned.

Processing can be set to occur automatically; a relatively early European case involving Google confirmed that operating a search

"Essentially, anything that happens to the data is likely to constitute processing. Even holding data at rest – sitting as a record in a database or stored in a library of hard copy documents – is considered processing of the data concerned."

facility to constantly scan the web and, in the process, collect personal data is, indeed, processing for the purpose of data protection legislation.[10]

Article 28 of the GDPR recognises the separate role that can exist where a separate data controller is responsible for the compliance of personal data that is made available to another party for processing. Activities that constitute processing are described above. An individual or organisation receiving personal data for processing from another party is expected to restrict its use of the data to the activities that it is instructed to undertake. Article 28 makes it clear that there must be a contract in place and, within that contract, clear instructions as to the scope of the processing activities to be undertaken.

The data processor is permitted to subcontract, but strict requirements apply here to ensure that a chain of responsibility for the personal data and acceptance of the limitations of use attached to the personal data are maintained.

III. The key data protection principles

1. Introduction

A number of key principles need to be followed to assure that an organisation is compliant with data protection rules.

The principles are found in Chapter 2 of the GDPR (Articles 5 to 11) and are, in summary, as follows:

- Accountability exists for all that is done with personal data by or under instructions from a data controller.
- The lawfulness, fairness and transparency in personal data retention and processing must be ensured.
- Personal data should be used only for declared purposes.
- Personal data held must be accurate and with systems in place to maintain up-to-date accuracy.
- The extent to which the personal data of any given individual is held within an organisation should be the minimum necessary for the purposes of that organisation.
- Personal data should be held for only as long as necessary, with active deletion procedures in place.
- Internal processes and duties placed on sub-processors must assure the integrity, confidentiality and security of personal data while being stored and when processed.

- Development of processes that involve the application of personal data must always be designed with the privacy of the data subject treated appropriately and in compliance with legislation.

2. Accountability for compliance

The principle of accountability is new to data protection in the sense that it was introduced by the EU GDPR. The accountability principle provides reinforcement to the other data protection principles that will be addressed in this chapter. Under the accountability duty:

- the data controller is responsible for the organisation's actions in the processing of personal data; and
- the data controller must be able to demonstrate the actions it has taken in order to ensure compliance with the other data protection principles.

In short, if a data controller fails in a compliance obligation, even if through an accidental omission, any argument that the failure is not significant is far less likely to impress the ICO if the organisation cannot provide evidence of the underlying governance procedures that it actively applies to meet the data protection principles.

In ICO guidance on this subject, organisations are exhorted to take this accountability requirement seriously, creating as it does an "opportunity for you to show, and prove, how you respect people's privacy".[11]

A key tool suggested by the ICO – applicable to larger organisations – is the development of a privacy management framework written in terms relevant to the organisation, its functions and how people and technology interact with personal data. A well-developed framework will provide for:

- controls over the systematic use of personal data within the organisation and by others under instructions from the organisation;
- reporting structures; and
- assessment and evaluation procedures.

A privacy management framework would highlight the policies the organisation is required to have in place, identifying ownership of these and frequency of reviews required, and specify both the authorisation levels for individuals to be provided with access to particular data sets and how data subject access requests and data breaches are to be managed in the organisation.

For smaller-scale organisations, the ICO also places emphasis on systems and procedures for data protection compliance, focusing, it is suggested, on:

- effective induction and ongoing training of staff to ensure understanding and awareness of the responsibilities that data protection compliance creates;
- comprehensive but proportionate policies and procedures for handling personal data; and
- high standards of record keeping.

It is important to also relate the accountability duty to Article 44(1) of the GDPR, which requires that:

- data controllers implement technical and organisational measures to ensure, and demonstrate, compliance with the GDPR;
- those measures be risk-based and proportionate; and
- those measures be regularly reviewed and updated.

3. Ensuring lawfulness, fairness and transparency
The lawful processing of personal data must always be undertaken in

"Organisations are exhorted to take this accountability requirement seriously."

circumstances permitted by Article 6 of the GDPR. The Article 6 requirements are discussed in Chapter VII.

The processing is unlawful (unless an exemption applies) if it is not possible to point to a lawful basis for the processing that was also, in a premeditated sense, taken to be the basis for the processing at the point at which the data is collected and, therefore, before the processing actually occurred.

Furthermore, for 'special category' data lawfulness is subject to the requirements of Article 9 also being satisfied. Special category data is addressed in Chapter VII where these additional criteria are examined.

Fairness in the way personal data is collected and used is a further requirement – data subjects must not be misled in the way their personal data is obtained, stored, processed and retained by the organisation. Privacy notices must be drafted with this in mind. It is always prudent to conduct a final review before publication to test out the concept: "Are we being fair in the way we are presenting this information?".

The duty to be transparent is the foundation for any privacy policy that an organisation develops, as well as for the manner in which it

"It is always prudent to conduct a final review before publication to test out the concept: 'Are we being fair in the way we are presenting this information?'."

responds to data subject access requests. Organisations should not overlook the different relationships that exist with individuals whose personal data is processed and how personal data is managed in these different relationships. A business with employees and both commercial and consumer customers will need to assess carefully its transparency duty – most likely having separate privacy notices so that the privacy policy for personal data concerning its employees[12] and that for data concerning customers are each developed compliantly and meet the transparency requirements of each particular audience.

4. Use of personal data for declared purposes

The scope of this duty should not be problematic. Personal data provided in circumstances in which the data subject knows that the data is to be processed to meet a specific function undertaken by the data controller can be processed in the manner contemplated, but should not be processed for other purposes not explicitly made known to the data subject. Since not all data processing needs to be based on consent, it is important to see this issue as a transparency issue with the scope of processing identified in the privacy notice being key to compliance.

A practice once prevalent involved the sale on commercial terms of customer lists. This is an example of a practice that is far more difficult to achieve when the declared purpose principle is taken into account.

5. Maintaining accuracy of personal data

It might appear at first sight that this duty can be complied with only on a basis that has the cooperation of the data subject insofar that personal data can only be as accurate as the provider makes it. If a data subject makes an error in, for example, providing a date of birth, usually the data controller can do little about that, save for having processes in place to provide data subjects with the opportunity to review and correct data periodically – a procedure to be encouraged since the accuracy duty also extends to keeping the data up to date "where necessary". 'Necessary', however, can be taken to be circumstances in which the information might or will change over time – such as an individual's credit rating, address or motor vehicle owned. A date of birth does not change; the data controller should therefore not be criticised for not having procedures in place to verify information that is not expected to change.

Matters are not so simplistic, unfortunately. In many cases personal data comes from third-party sources, meaning that the data subject has not taken personal responsibility for its accuracy at the point of transfer.

The duty of the recipient data controller is generally taken to be one that places a positive obligation on the data controller to take active steps to correct personal data that is known not to be accurate. The duty does not appear to extend so far as to have every item of personal data received from a third-party source verified by the data subject. The approach to be taken to rectification of personal data that is inaccurate is discussed in more detail in Chapter XI.

6. Keeping personal data to a minimum

Under the GDPR, organisations are required to ensure that personal data held is adequate, relevant and limited to the personal data that is necessary for the purposes for which the data is processed.

It is recommended that an organisation review the detail of personal data collected through a process of audit while assessing its data policy compliance; this would cover all processes under which personal data is captured or brought into the organisation under arrangements with third parties.

Case study

Keeping personal data to a minimum

A recruitment agency encourages potential candidates to provide information that enables the agency to promote the candidate to potential employers. A very minimal data set is required – leaving it to the candidate to remain in control of the much more detailed information that a CV would contain. One information field that must be filled in is 'university attended'. When asked about how this information is used, the data controller admits that it is requested because, at some stage, the collation of statistics associated with job locations and university location has been considered. But this has never been followed through – meaning that there is no legitimate reason for collecting and holding this element of personal data.

The process of data minimisation extends to other aspects of the processing of personal data – something that is often overlooked. The extent to which the data controller limits the processing of personal data to circumstances that are compliant should also be given weight, with internal protections in place to control access. For example, many will have been frustrated when speaking to call centres and being unable to provide a last piece of requested personal identification information that has been requested by the call centre handler. The inability of the call handler to be flexible over the issue is probably evidence of strong systems being in place – with the call handler unable to access your data unless you have played a complete part in authorising the access by providing the necessary identification information.

"It is recommended that an organisation review the detail of personal data collected through a process of audit while assessing its data policy compliance."

7. Storing personal data for only as long as necessary

To understand this duty involves considering what is meant by 'necessary' and the options (some not obvious) relating to how the data controller can deal with personal data with this duty in mind.

Care needs to be taken where there are other reasons for retaining personal data, as is explained below.

In the context of data protection legislation, the term 'necessary' has been scrutinised and developed through numerous legal proceedings. The leading case, *Huber v Republic of Germany*,[13] led to the Court of Justice of the European Union setting out an expectation that, in making a decision, the data controller is expected to adopt the least restrictive approach (from the data subject's point of view) to meeting the end requirement.

So, must a data controller delete personal data that, in the particular circumstances, no longer meets the threshold test for being retained on a necessary basis? A data controller may, in fact, take several approaches:

- delete the data;
- destroy the data (eg, where the data is held in paper format);

- pseudonymise the data; or
- anonymise the data.

The status of personal data held under this necessity principle can change over time. Certain data elements may be required and, therefore, necessary to fulfil obligations owed to a data subject over a long-term business relationship, whereas other information – for example, to carry out an initial credit check that is not to be repeated – should under this principle be securely deleted under the organisation's policy for data retention, which will also be a key compliance tool to meet the data minimisation obligation.

As is to be expected, there are qualifications to the rule that personal data must be deleted or destroyed in line with a declared data deletion policy. Specific periods should be adopted for particular categories of data based on legal or other considerations. Table 2 gives the most obvious examples, but specific trades and professions will create additional circumstances in which data retention periods must be observed.

Table 2. Requirements and retention periods

Requirement	Retention period that should be observed
Potential litigation – not personal injury	6 years, or 12 in relation to issues arising from arrangements created under execution of an agreement or other legal document as a deed
Potential litigation – personal injury	3 years – this being the limitation period for claims
Recruitment records for unsuccessful candidate	3 months – this being the period in which discrimination-related complaints may be brought
Contact details for COVID-19 tracing	A requirement brought in to support test-and-trace processes requiring details to be retained for 14 days

Case study

When personal data is difficult to delete

An interesting case[14] of unlawful data retention concerned a Danish taxi company that was found, during a data protection inspection, to have a practice of recording details of taxi trips that included the customer's name, telephone number and details of the trip (obviously including addresses involved). The company deleted the customer's name after two years but retained the remaining data for five years.

As a telephone number retained by a data controller enables identification of the individual, the company was considered to still be holding the personal data of the customer.

When asked about the practice, the company argued that its IT system did not readily provide for deletion of the telephone number. The Danish Data Protection Authority, however, opined that it is not acceptable to retain data longer than necessary only because the company's system makes compliance with the GDPR burdensome.

8. Integrity, confidentiality and security

This principle embraces a number of considerations associated with the ability of the data controller or data processor to ensure that personal data is held securely, accessed only as and when necessary by employees and others with security considerations requiring that the organisation understands the potential role of various technical measures that can be taken, including encryption, the effective use of firewalls and testing regimes (often referred to as 'penetration testing') to identify weaknesses in the area of cyber security, and applies these effectively.

It is timely to mention that data protection is not just about the way data is accessed and used, but also about maintaining the data and not losing access to it. If the sole repository for an individual's personal data was a computer hard drive and that hard drive is destroyed – for example, in a fire – then that is a notifiable loss of personal data that may be adjudged a breach if the surrounding circumstances demonstrate compliance failures (eg, in the procedures enabling back-up of the data). Data subjects are entitled to have their data maintained so that they enjoy the actual benefits of the data controller's intentions to use the personal data concerned for the benefit of that data subject.

A further point that can be overlooked is that the data controller cannot adopt an 'out of sight, out of mind' attitude to circumstances in which the processing of data is contracted out. Appropriate due diligence must be undertaken to ensure that the processor also meets

"The data controller cannot adopt an 'out of sight, out of mind' attitude to circumstances in which the processing of data is contracted out."

the requirements of this principle before that processor is instructed to deal with the personal data on behalf of the data controller. This requirement is explained in detail in Chapter V.

9. Privacy by design

Data controllers must, when undertaking any project that leads to or involves the processing of personal data, ensure that their processes are developed in a manner that is compliant with Article 25 of the GDPR, which is known as the 'privacy by design' principle.

Article 25 specifically requires that:

- appropriate technical and organisation measures be implemented to minimise risk of harm to the data subject; and
- the quantity of data concerning a data subject collected and then subjected to particular processing operations be limited, with emphasis also on the data being held for a limited period of time and controls being in place regarding who in an organisation can access the information.

10. Principles applicable to processors

When the EU GDPR was introduced in 2018, a new approach was adopted relating to the role of data processors processing personal data under the instructions of the data controller. Previously, a party processing data that it did not have legal control over was subject to very limited legal duties. A series of legal duties is now imposed on data processors.

The duties arise both directly from the activities of the data processor and indirectly from the robust rights accorded to data subjects in respect of the processing of personal data, as will be explained.

We will see in Chapter V that data controllers must formalise the relationship with the data processor in a clear, documented manner. At the core of the data processor's responsibilities is the duty to process the personal data that is available to it strictly in accordance with the documented instructions of the data controller.[15]

The data processor must act accordingly or it will be in breach of data protection legislation in the following two situations:

- The data processor fails to act compliantly with the instructions of the data controller. This could, for example, be circumstances in which the data processor is required to delete certain data following its processing; and
- The data processor acts outside of the scope of its instructions. This might be by taking advantage of the access it has to the personal data and subsequently processing the data in a manner that is in its interest and therefore going beyond the scope of the instructions provided.

The data processor's indirect liability arises from the GDPR provisions making the data processor jointly and severally liable to the data subject in connection with any unlawful processing of personal data. The aim is to maximise the ability of a data subject to recover compensation in circumstances of a data breach.

Data controllers and data processors should in their contract provide for re-allocation of responsibility for actions or omissions of the data controller through an appropriately drafted indemnity clause. The issue becomes more difficult for the data processor should the data controller become insolvent.

Data processors are required to register with the ICO and are subject to the requirements of Chapter 4 of the GDPR that are relevant to and place duties on those processing personal data.

IV. Demonstrating that processing is lawful

1. Introduction

The processing of personal data by or on behalf of the data controller is, in practice, regulated through the principle of lawful purpose – the legal justification for undertaking the processing. When special category data is processed there are further considerations – additional protections for the rights of data subjects given the sensitivities around that kind of data. Special category data and protections for that data are explained in Chapter VII.

The GDPR presents the data controller with several justifications that can, when correctly adopted, assure that the processing undertaken is lawful. If an incorrect basis is adopted or a basis relied upon does not in practice meet the necessary requirements associated with its use (explained below), then the processing will not satisfy the lawfulness test.

In addition, data subjects can, with some limitations, exercise their right to restrict processing by requiring that the processing that the data controller intends to make should not take place, even though the data is held lawfully by the data controller.[16]

Table 3 provides a summary of the lawful purposes that legitimise processing, and an explanation of the requirements that need to be met before the entitlement to process is taken advantage of.

Table 3. Lawful purposes legitimising processing and requirements to take into account

Basis for legitimate processing	Qualifications or criteria to be taken into account
Consent	The consent must be freely given, specific, informed and unambiguous. There are particular requirements for consent to be given by children, explained in Chapter VIII.
Necessary to prepare and/or perform a contract with the data subject	The data controller should be able to demonstrate that actions taken with a view to entering into a contract with the data subject (eg, providing a quotation) and then performing the contract could not be carried out without use of the personal data in the manner proposed.
Necessary to comply with a legal obligation	The data controller must be under an obligation to process the data – this may be through a legislative requirement such as PAYE reporting to HMRC or guidance having statutory effect.
Necessary to protect the vital interests of the data subject	Protection of the health of the data subject will permit the processing. It is possible, but unclear, whether protection of an individual's personal property (eg, a lost mobile phone) would also enable the processing.
Necessary to perform a task carried out in the public interest	The public authority seeking to take advantage of this basis for processing is required to demonstrate that some lawful authority exists entitling the authority to process the personal data in a particular way.
Necessary in the pursuit of the legitimate interests of the data controller	While this is broadly specified for each situation in which the data controller wishes to process the personal data – the reference to 'necessary' being key – there is also a proportionality test. This requires the data controller to demonstrate that the fundamental rights and freedoms of the individual will not be overridden by the processing activity involved.

2. Some examples of the application of the lawful purpose test

2.1 Consent

Obtaining the consent of the data subject may seem a relatively straightforward gate to pass through in demonstrating that processing is lawful.

The process of obtaining consent must, however, be seen in the context of the principle of fairness that was examined in Chapter III. The process under which personal data is obtained must be one that enables the data subject to be as aware as possible of all the consequences of the data being shared with the data controller. A case arising under the Data Protection Act 1986 remains one of the landmark cases on the subject.[17] After responding to newspaper advertisements and placing orders with a retailer, individuals were told that their data would be sold on to third parties on a commercial basis. The case went to court and a determination was made that individuals should be allowed to assume that no use would be made of their personal data other than for the purposes of servicing the order placed with the original retailer and other purposes permitted by data protection legislation without a consent requirement.[18]

"The process under which personal data is obtained must be one that enables the data subject to be as aware as possible of all the consequences of the data being shared with the data controller."

In order to ensure that the consent is given freely, the giving of the consent must be explicitly separated from anything else that the individual is required to do. Thus, when ordering goods over the internet a tick box requirement to confirm that terms and conditions of sale are agreed to cannot also include the consent for data processing for marketing purposes. Note that the supplier will rely on the 'in order to perform a contract' test to process the personal data when received; therefore, the consent is, in effect, required only for marketing purposes!

Consent must be given through a positive act on the part of the data subject – this making clear that tick-the-box style opt-in/opt-out procedures must allow for opt-in by default. Pre-ticking the box is not permitted.

Further points to note concerning consent are that there must be an ability to subsequently withdraw the consent and the consent must be documented, with the data controller expected to provide evidence that consent was given in any given circumstances.

Case study

Keeping consents granular

An online retailer may have a facility enabling the data subject to expressly agree to information being held in order to generate an email when an item the data subject is interested in, but which is out of stock, becomes available for ordering. The data subject may also be invited to sign up for regular newsletters and special offers. These are two distinct circumstances in which consent is required and they should therefore be provided for separately, through separate tick-the-box procedures.

2.2 Preparing for and performing a contract

This basis for lawful processing comprises two elements. In chronological order, these are as follows:

- The data subject has requested that certain steps be taken before it enters into a contract; and
- The processing is necessary for the performance of the contract.

The data subject must be a party to the contract. The requirements stop short, however, of demanding that the data controller be also a party to the same contract, meaning that more complex relationships can be accommodated – such as when a third party provides finance for a purchase transaction but must first carry out credit checks.

Employers should usually rely on this basis for lawful processing rather than rely on consent, on the grounds that it may be difficult to demonstrate that consent was given 'freely' by an employee. As the employee will be under a contract of employment, this approach is appropriate. It will enable details to be passed to a specialist payroll processing business and include processing of the employee's bank account details.

2.3 Legal obligation

Staying with the employer/employee relationship, an employer is under a duty to pass information to HMRC as the taxation authority. In many situations, requirements to undertake money laundering checks will form the basis for this type of processing.

Note the reference to obligation. It is insufficient for any data controller to attempt to apply this approach in circumstances where there may be a statutory function to be discharged but the function is not expressed to be an actual obligation on the data controller.

2.4 Vital interests

Sensibly, disclosure of personal data is permitted in circumstances in which the vital interests of the data subject may otherwise be compromised, such as in the following examples:

- A parent has provided a school with guidance on how to deal with a rare medical condition that could occur while their child is in school. The circumstances arise and the school passes the information to a paramedic attending the incident.
- Police are investigating the disappearance of an elderly person suffering from dementia. They may request access to CCTV footage held by a local bus operator.

2.5 Performance of public functions

There are numerous circumstances in which legal requirements are placed on public bodies to process personal data. Notably, in the course of performing their functions public authorities should not rely on legitimate interest as the lawful purpose for processing data – this basis is withheld in consequence of the fact that the government can determine in very clear terms when and in what circumstances personal data may be processed.

Examples include the duty of a primary school to transfer particular data concerning a pupil on to the pupil's secondary school; the processing of data in circumstances in which a notifiable disease has been contracted; and for the purpose of maintaining a register of electors. Note that in the latter case, publication of the personal data must be undertaken with an opt-out right for the public version of the register following a challenge to the previous practice of the full register being published.[19]

2.6 Legitimate interests

This provision is intended to support processing of personal data undertaken in ordinary business circumstances where the processing is of data that is lawfully held by the data controller and should be regarded as a legitimate use of the data in circumstances in which the data subject is not affected by an overriding of the fundamental rights and freedoms of the individual.

To give a benign example, the processing of personal data to create back-up copies of the data would be an appropriate application of this lawful purpose. Likewise, passing information to a debt collection agency would satisfy the criterion if a debt was genuinely owed and overdue for payment. The retention of call records in a call centre would be another appropriate circumstance.

The application of the legitimate interests principle makes it appropriate for a business to send marketing-focused emails to a data subject where business has been transacted with that person, provided the subject matter is associated with the item purchased.

V. What it means to be a data controller or processor

1. What it means to be a data controller

The criteria that determine whether an organisation has the status of data controller for any given circumstances in which it has access to personal data is explained in Chapter II.

By way of reminder, the two functions that are central to determining whether an organisation is a data controller are as follows:

- The organisation decides what personal data it collects and holds, and it thereafter manages the data falling into its controlling role; and
- The organisation processes the personal data as its own decisions and not under the instructions of another – the concept of processing including how the personal data is initially taken into the organisation and stored by either the data controller or another party under the data controller's instructions.

2. Responsibilities as a data controller

Being clear as to circumstances in which an organisation has the status of data controller is generally a relatively straightforward matter. Here is an example:

- An organisation that specialises in mail order fulfilment will be receiving personal data from the organisation that is undertaking some form of marketing activity to print and despatch the mailshot concerned. It is using the personal data supplied in a processor capacity. It may hold the personal data on its system for a period of time – this is an example of a matter that the data controller should agree as part of the data processing arrangement. But that will not make it a controller of the data as it holds the data only by reason of the instructions from the mail order business.
- The mail order business, by contrast, is the one that makes the decision to instruct the fulfilment business to process the data in exactly the way the fulfilment business then does process the data; the mail order business is therefore the party with the responsibilities outlined above (ie, it collects, holds and manages the data, and decides how to process it).

Later in this report we look in more detail at the concept of instructions that pass from a data controller to a data processor, but what will be clear from the above is that the processor is able to process the data only under the data controller's instructions.

"The data collection is a necessary part of the relationship with the individual – for example, the individual might be an employee or in a contract with the organisation."

A number of criteria can be used to test out whether the role of an organisation as data controller is being performed. In its guide to the UK GDPR,[20] the ICO lists the characteristics that it will look for should it need to make any kind of determination relating to an organisation's responsibility for personal data. The key criteria are whether the organisation is:

- taking responsibility for the collection and the processing that is undertaken;
- deciding the purposes of and intended outcomes from any processing;
- deciding what personal data should be collected; and
- deciding which individuals the collection activity relates to.

The data collection is a necessary part of the relationship with the individual – for example, the individual might be an employee or in a contract with the organisation.

The ICO will also look at other considerations, such as whether the processing activities undertaken by or on behalf of the data controller are on a for-profit basis, whether decisions are taken about the individual based upon the personal data processed and whether there is autonomy in the way and extent to which processing takes place.

3. When will a joint controller relationship come into existence?
This is an important question when personal data passes from one party to another, and the ultimate recipient's agreed role extends beyond processing the personal data under the instructions of the data's original recipient.

The concept of joint controller is provided for by Article 26 of the GDPR. The characteristics to consider will include:

- whether the parties have a common outcome planned for the processing of the personal data;
- whether the parties have access to a common database that contains the relevant personal data; and
- whether the data processing activities are jointly planned.

Case study
An example of a joint controller relationship
An employer has a number of employees following a particular apprenticeship programme. The employer has appointed a training provider to manage the educational and training inputs required within the apprenticeship programme. The progress of the apprentices accordingly requires inputs from both the employer and the training provider.

A common outcome is clearly planned in terms of an expectation that an accurate record will be maintained concerning the apprentices' progress and a common database is maintained. There is also joint planning of the processing as each of the employer and the training provider must have a coordinated approach to the overall management of the database.

4. Responsibilities when processing personal data

The scope of the term 'processing' was explained in Chapter II.

Keep in mind at the outset that processing can be undertaken by the data controller or by a party instructed to undertake the processing. In each case there are responsibilities under data protection legislation to be taken into account.

The legal duties associated with controlling personal data cannot be delegated to another, but the processing of that data can be, provided that a significant number of requirements (listed in Article 28 of the GDPR) are complied with.

5. Overview of the process of appointing a data processor

The GDPR incorporates a number of mandatory requirements that a data controller must follow when appointing a data processor.

To be compliant, the process of appointing a third party to undertake data processing on behalf of the data controller involves the following:

- Ensuring that the decision to appoint a sub-processor is transparent. Data subjects are entitled to be aware of the intention to appoint such a sub-processor – therefore, the matter needs to be addressed in the organisation's privacy notice;
- Following due diligence practices to assess the appropriateness in appointing a given third party as a sub-processor;
- Agreeing within the commercial terms covering the appointment of the sub-processor terms and conditions that are mandatory requirements imposed by Article 28(4) of the GDPR; and
- Pro-actively monitoring the performance of the processor's duties on a continuing basis throughout the period in which the instructions to process data are in place.

6. Satisfying the duty of transparency

The requirements to be taken into account when drafting a privacy notice are covered in Chapter VI. Details of the identity of processors should be included with access to the equivalent privacy notices of processors facilitated – this is usually by way of the incorporation of a web link (directed to the processor's privacy notice) within the notice of the data controller.

"The legal duties associated with controlling personal data cannot be delegated to another, but the processing of that data can be, provided that a significant number of requirements are complied with."

7. Applying due diligence in order to assess appropriateness in the appointment

The GDPR presents data controllers with a duty to ascertain that, when appointing a sub-processor:

- the sub-processor has the capability to carry out its processing obligations in a manner that safeguards the personal data made available to it for processing; and
- the sub-processor has the ability to give 'sufficient guarantees' relating to technical and security precautions that will address and protect the data subject.

8. An example due diligence checklist

The core questions to be included in a due diligence questionnaire are set out in Table 4. There will be other matters requiring scrutiny on a more commercial basis – for instance, whether the sub-processor also acts for competitors or has any other conflict of interest, whether a service level agreement is in place that underpins performance commitments and whether the organisation subscribes to any codes of practice or certification schemes, recognised under the GDPR, that encourage the development of such codes or schemes.[21]

Table 4. Due diligence checklist

Due diligence subject	Checked and relevant information/documentation obtained: Yes/No
Details of any accreditations held (eg, ISO27001)	
Technical systems in place including encryption methodologies	
How the personal data will be held and methods for access to the data controlled	
Details of any further sub-processing (eg, use of a third-party data centre)	
Details of staff training both at induction and on an ongoing basis	
The processor has an appointed DPO or can identify another individual with responsibility (providing details of the qualifications and experience of the individual)	
The processor will agree in its contract with the data controller to commit to the mandatory requirements of Article 28 of the GDPR concerning appointment of a sub-processor	

9. Agreeing commercial terms

The data controller is required to ensure that it has a contract with the data processor. The contract must set out the subject matter and duration of the processing required, the nature and purpose of the processing, the types of personal data and the categories of data subjects together with understandings regarding the obligations and rights of the appointed data controller.

Under Article 28(3) of the GDPR, there are specific requirements to be incorporated into the contract. In summary, these are that the sub-processor must:

- act only on the written instructions of the controller;
- ensure that people processing the data are subject to a duty of confidence;
- take appropriate measures to ensure the security of processing;

- engage sub-processors only with the prior consent of the controller and under a written contract;
- assist the controller in providing subject access and allowing data subjects to exercise their rights under the GDPR;
- assist the controller in meeting its GDPR obligations in relation to the security of processing, the notification of personal data breaches and data protection impact assessments;
- delete or return all personal data to the controller as requested at the end of the contract; and
- submit to audits and inspections, provide the controller with whatever information it needs to ensure that they are both meeting their Article 28 obligations, and tell the controller immediately if it is asked to do something infringing the GDPR or any provisions of the Data Protection Act 2018.

10. Engaging sub-processors internationally

Where sub-processing involves a transfer of personal data outside of the UK, it has already been determined by the UK, through an adequacy decision,[22] that the member states of the EU and EEA, through their adherence to the EU GDPR, provide appropriate protection for personal data of UK citizens that may be transferred into any of these territories for processing. It will be necessary to

"The data controller is required to ensure that it has a contract with the data processor. The contract must set out the subject matter and duration of the processing required, the nature and purpose of the processing, the types of personal data and the categories of data subjects together with understandings regarding the obligations and rights of the appointed data controller."

follow the requirements of the GDPR in making the appointment, but no further steps are required. Where the appointment of a processor involves transfer of the personal data to any other country (unless it is one for which the UK has made an adequacy determination), additional steps are required – as will be explained in Chapter XIV.

11. Processing in a group of companies

An issue under frequent consideration is whether transfers of personal data within a group of companies need to be documented. A group, for this purpose, will comprise a legal entity that holds ownership of at least one subsidiary company. Any companies in further tiers below that level will also need to be controlled if they are to be classified as subsidiaries under company law.

When considering the position of a group of companies, Recital 37 of the EU GDPR makes it clear that data protection compliance across a group of companies is the responsibility of the ultimate holding company.

Which companies fall under the responsibility of a particular entity in terms of data protection will depend on particular criteria associated with ownership, financial participation and the existence of control over the affairs of the entity concerned.

The GDPR is silent on the need for intra-group data processing agreements or data sharing agreements. It would probably be good practice nonetheless to take such steps (ie, have data processing or data sharing agreements in place, particularly where the transfer is into a territory that does not benefit from an adequacy decision) as part of the process of accountability – assuring, as it will do, a recognition within all group companies of the importance of data protection compliance.

VI. Transparency – how to draft privacy notices

1. Introduction

At the heart of data protection law is the transparency duty. This must be satisfied by all data controllers and data processors.

The concept of transparency is wide ranging: most obviously, and the subject of this chapter, the requirement to allow data subjects to see how data controllers deal with their personal data. But it is also about data subject requests – allowing the data subject to understand what information is being held and thereby enabling the data subject to make informed requests concerning the personal data controlled by that data controller.

This chapter concentrates on privacy, sometimes also called fair processing, notices.

Every data controller that holds a data subject's personal data is required to demonstrate how it obtains and then manages and processes that personal data. This leads to our being confronted daily, sometimes on multiple occasions, with an invitation to review a privacy notice.

This, inevitably, leads in turn to privacy notice fatigue – very evident when the GDPR had its big bang day in May 2018 with a flurry of updated privacy notices hitting inboxes and mail boxes, many of them as a last minute exercise.

The concept of privacy notice fatigue is not lost on the ICO. In a sense, the legislation has made the data protection environment that we live in susceptible to that fatigue. There are numerous specific requirements laid down by the GDPR[23] aimed at providing as much transparency as possible for the benefit of the data subject.

In consequence, a great many privacy notices are presented in a dense format defaulting to text that would be regarded as legalese, making the contents difficult to understand by a lay person.

The ICO provides guidance on how an organisation should develop and then publish privacy notices in a user-friendly way.[24]

2. Developing a data privacy notice

At this point we need to take a look at one of the most fundamental issues faced by an organisation about to start collecting personal data: there should be no collection of personal data without first providing a data subject with an understanding of why that data is being requested and what will happen to it. It is irrelevant whether the data subject does then scrutinise the privacy notice – access to it must be available at the point of collection in order for the fairness duty to be satisfied.

That said, a common misunderstanding is that it is necessary to present the data subject with the full privacy policy at each point when data is being collected. The ICO is very keen to see what we could call 'user-friendly strategies' where, at the point at which a specific item of information is requested – for example, a telephone number – there is a link to a specific information point that explains "we need your telephone number because we might need to contact you concerning your child's welfare", to give one example. The statement must be honest and comprehensive and must, in turn, guide the user to the full privacy notice in case the data subject would like to learn more about data processing procedures.

An example of this approach might be as follows – taken from a web page requesting details from the data subject:

Telephone: [ ] *why we request this information*

When preparing to draft a privacy notice, a good starting point will always be to consider where the personal data collected comes from. There are four distinct sources that may be relevant and need to be referenced in the privacy notice:

"When preparing to draft a privacy notice, a good starting point will always be to consider where the personal data collected comes from."

- information volunteered by the data subject – although 'volunteered' may not be the correct term in some cases (more on that below);
- information that the data subject provides not through an input to a form or the like, but through the data collector's interrogation of the data subject's computer using cookies;
- information that the data subject consents to being accessed by the data controller, but which needs to be accessed from a third party that in turn gives permission to the data controller to access the information – for example, a credit score file held by a specialist company; and
- more controversially, and now not permitted by data protection law other than in the case of law enforcement and for surveillance purposes, information obtained without consent from other sources and which is possible in consequence of access to particular elements of personal data available to the data controller with sources of other information, such as a Facebook or Amazon account.

The fourth point is made for a reason – that is, to emphasise the importance of a privacy notice being comprehensive in setting out exactly what information is being taken from other sources. If the notice is not comprehensive, data collected outside of the stated sources and detail of information collected will have been taken in breach of data protection laws.

3. Developing a privacy notice from scratch

Good practice in developing a privacy notice can be achieved by using a checklist that covers the requirements set out in Article 13 of the GDPR. The checklist would thus include:

- who you are;
- the types of personal data that you collect;
- how you obtain that personal data;
- why you want to have that personal data and hold a copy of it;
- how you use the information;
- the legal basis relied upon for the processing activities you engage in;
- who you may share the data with;
- how you apply additional safeguards if data is transferred outside of the EEA to a territory that is not regarded as 'adequate' in its data protection;
- how the information is stored and an explanation of your organisation's security measures;
- how long data is stored for;
- a statement of the rights available to the data subject in connection with data held (see Chapter XI) and how the rights may be exercised; and
- how to raise issues or questions with the data controller and how to contact the ICO if the data subject has concerns.

A well-drafted privacy notice is like a route map – starting with who the data controller is and then, as will be clear from the list above, taking the data subject whose data is about to be collected through the processing that may occur to collected data. There are points to take care of in the way the notice is developed.

4. My privacy notice – am I making the position clear?

Always ask this question when you think the exercise is complete. The legal duty of transparency extends to ensuring that information provided is comprehensible to the reader. It is helpful to test a proposed notice out on a number of lay people to gauge their reaction.

Particular care now needs to be taken in the case of children who are entitled to have the benefit of detail within a privacy notice being presented in an easy-to-understand manner. This aspect is covered in Chapter VIII.

5. Do I need different notices for different circumstances?

By far the best-known type of privacy notice is that accessible from an organisation's website. Such notice will address the implications for any personal data that the website visitor shares with the promoter of the website. The notice should address individuals making general enquiries of the organisation, subscribing to receive newsletters and entering into e-commerce transactions with that party.

Behind the scenes, however, there will be other activities of the organisation involving the processing of personal data and, therefore, further requirements to provide a privacy notice.

Where an organisation has employees, their personal data requires to be addressed through an appropriate notice. That notice may also extend to covering recruitment activities, given that individuals share personal data when seeking employment.

Public authorities must also address requirements specific to the personal data that is processed as part of their responsibilities. In education, notices relating to student data and data held concerning parents/carers must be put in place.

In the same fashion, the NHS and private hospitals will be expected to have privacy notices appropriate to their circumstances. COVID-19 presents us with a situation in which new requirements for access to and processing of personal data has become a significant issue.

Local authorities are presented with probably the greatest challenge in terms of managing compliance, given the multitude of different functions that a typical local authority will perform – many requiring a privacy notice addressing the processing undertaken in connection with the function concerned.

6. Creating a privacy notice – tracking the data journey

An effective way of understanding how personal data is brought into an organisation and then processed is to carry out a data mapping exercise: setting out in chronological order how an individual interacts with the organisation, sometimes providing a little personal data at an early point in the relationship but thereafter providing more data, with that data frequently having greater sensitivity – for instance, providing payment information in the form of credit card details. Below is an example in graphical format of how a number of key points to feature in a privacy notice can be captured and then re-presented effectively in that notice. The exercise will also be helpful in informing the development of a register of data sets that the organisation holds.

The example in Figure 1 reflects how an app designed to provide social media-related functionality for the benefit of the user receives and facilitates the processing of the user's personal data.

Figure 1. The data journey

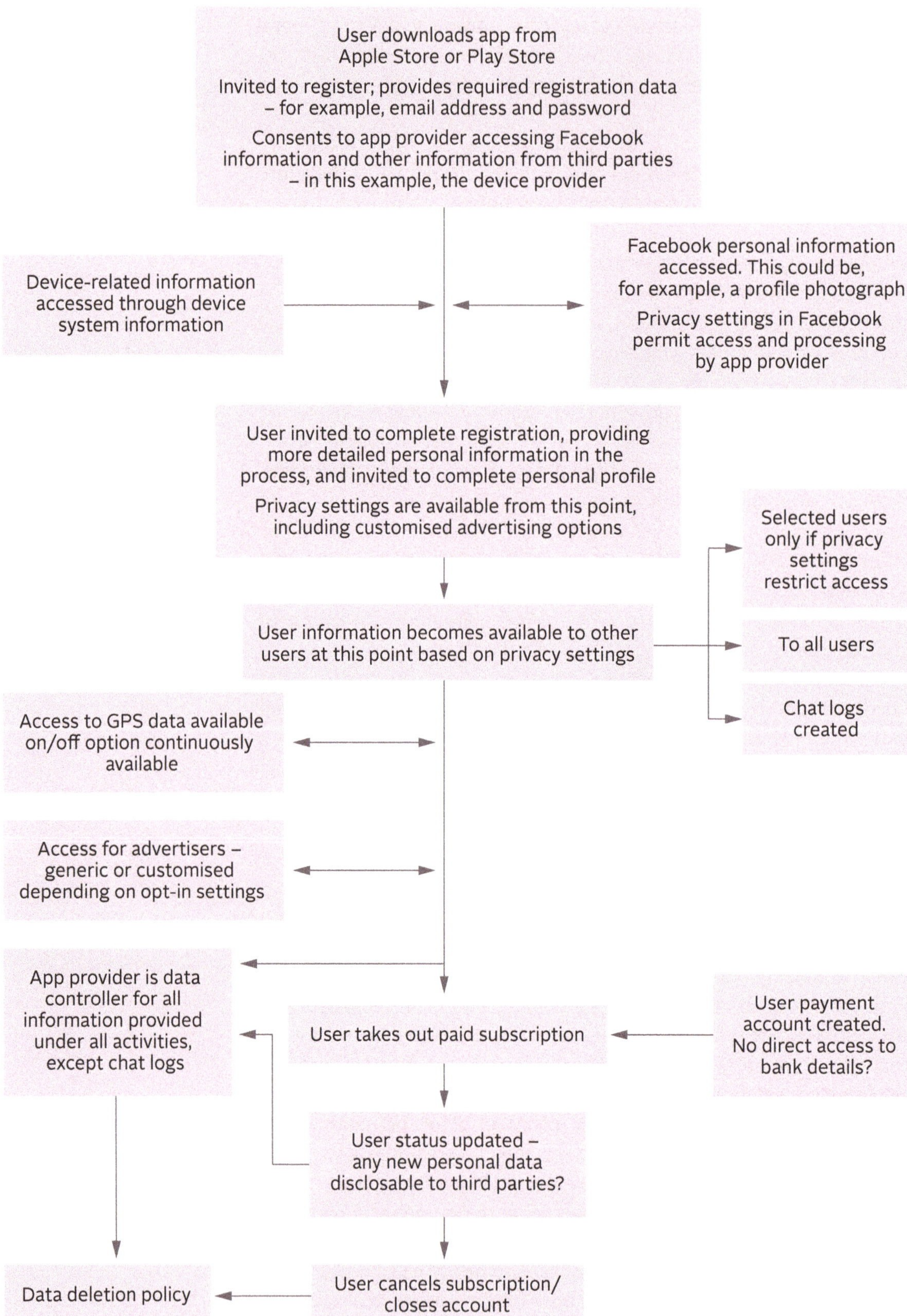

VII. What's special about 'special category' data?

1. Introduction

The term 'special category' data was introduced by the EU GDPR. With that introduction came requirements that there must be an appropriate justification for both holding the data and then further processing the data in order to ensure that data controllers regard data of this kind as needing particular care. This chapter provides an explanation as to what constitutes special category data, and what the data controller must satisfy by law when it intends to hold and undertake other processing of that data.

2. What constitutes special category data?

The following types of data are identified as 'special category' under Article 9(1) of the GDPR:

- data disclosing racial or ethnic origin;
- data identifying political opinions;
- data associated with religious or philosophical beliefs;
- data establishing membership of a trade union;
- biological data of a genetic nature;
- biometric data;
- data associated with a person's health, including mental wellbeing; and
- data identifying sex life or sexual orientation.

The principle of special treatment existed before the coming into force of the EU GDPR, although under the 1995 directive the term used was 'sensitive personal data'.

Under that directive, data relating to criminal convictions fell within the sensitive personal data category, but under the GDPR, such data is not regulated by the special category regime. How criminal data is dealt with now is explained later in this chapter.

It is worth noting that while a list as set out above provides welcome certainty, it also creates the risk of missing other examples of personal data which, for different reasons, could be regarded as sufficiently sensitive to be accorded the same status. This point has been picked up in the context of education by the Department for Education in its Schools GDPR Toolkit,[25] noting that other data handled by schools should be controlled with particular care. Eligibility for free school meals is given as one example.

3. Additional requirements for processing special category data

It is important to appreciate that the requirements below must be satisfied, where relevant, in addition to the data controller having an elementary lawful basis for processing the data, as required by Article 6 of the GDPR. By way of example, the processing through an

"Under the GDPR, data relating to criminal convictions is not regulated by the special category regime."

online booking system of a hotel reservation for a guest who has a requirement for wheelchair-friendly facilities will involve processing by the hotel in preparation to perform a contract (providing accommodation) and the processing of personal data that identifies the guest as having a disability.

The GDPR requires the data controller to have also considered the additional requirements of Article 9 to the extent that these are relevant to the processing activity to be undertaken.

There are no fewer than 10 particular grounds which can form the basis for the processing of special category personal data. Each is explained briefly below.

3.1 Explicit consent (a test requiring a higher standard of care than a basic consent) has been provided by the data subject

The data subject should, when consenting, be provided with information that highlights the categories of special category data that are to be processed. The data controller may subsequently need to demonstrate not only that the consent was freely given, but also that the balance of interests between the parties had been considered with due weight given to any risk that the data subject's interests could be detrimentally affected. Where a particular service will not be provided to the data subject unless consent is given, careful consideration is required; if available, a different approach to the processing of the personal data (one of the other options explained below) should be used.

3.2 An employer/employee relationship basis under which processing for employment, social security or other social-related legislation or in observance of collective agreement with a trade union

The ambit of this provision is associated with:

- employment law;
- social security law; and
- laws relating to social protection.

Where an employer can point to legislative requirements within any of these categories, the processing is lawful. However, the employer must at the same time have an appropriately developed policy in place. This can be seen as the means by which the Article 9(2)(b) requirement that the employer provide "the appropriate safeguards for the fundamental rights and interests of the data subject" are in place and adopted. The development of an appropriately worded staff privacy notice will typically be the vehicle to demonstrate compliance.

"Recital 46 of the EU GDPR provides useful clarification of the legislative intent, suggesting that the processing should occur in circumstances in which the interest to be protected is 'essential for the life of the data subject or that of another natural person'."

3.3 Processing is to protect the vital interests of the data subject or another person and can be considered necessary in the particular circumstances

To apply, this provision must meet two criteria.

First, the processing must be 'necessary', which occurs when the data controller has concluded (correctly based on evidence available) that the individual is unable, physically or legally, to consent to the processing.

Secondly, the processing must be associated with the 'vital interests' of the data subject or some other person.

In the previous iteration of this provision under the Data Protection Act 1998, the ICO published guidance attempting to assist decision-making in this area. Examples cited as appropriate included medical emergencies. The EU GDPR addresses this issue in Recital 46. The recital provides useful clarification of the legislative intent, suggesting that the processing should occur in circumstances in which the interest to be protected is "essential for the life of the data subject or that of another natural person".

There is some continuing debate about whether vital interests must be narrowly construed and involve consideration only of physical or mental risks to the person, or whether risks to other property that can somehow be regarded as a 'vital' interest should be taken to allow such processing.

If in interpretation of the UK GDPR we continue to follow Recital 46 of the EU GDPR, the narrower construction appears most appropriate.

3.4 Processing by a not-for-profit body in the course of its legitimate activities

Organisations that are entitled to take advantage of this basis for processing must either have the status of being established for purposes that are political, philosophical or religious, or be a trade union.

The processing that must be undertaken is specifically limited to processing for the purposes of the organisation only; in other words, processing is limited to data subjects who are members, former members and individuals who have regular contact with the organisation, and to processing operations that are internal to the organisation.

3.5 Processing concerns personal data that is, effectively, in the public domain due to an action of the data subject or authorised by the data subject

Where special category data has been made public by the data subject, the processing of that personal data may be carried out lawfully without any specific consent from the data subject. The circumstances in which information has come into the public domain need to be carefully considered to ensure that there is a clear link between the data coming into the public domain and the actions of the data subject (or someone on the data subject's behalf) to cause that to have occurred.

3.6 Processing is necessary in order to establish, exercise or defend a legal claim

There are many circumstances in which a legal right cannot be pursued or a claim defended without the processing of special category data. This, accordingly, has been provided for, but very specifically associated with judicial proceedings. The transfer of data from an insurance company to its legal advisers associated with the defence of a legal claim made by a third party would be an example of circumstances that are provided for.

Activities associated with presenting information to a legal adviser for advice on a possible claim would also be permitted. Advice required in any circumstances not involving possible judicial proceedings would not be an appropriate basis for processing. Legal advisers dealing with special category data in other circumstances would need to be able to rely on Article 6 grounds, such as in order to perform a contract where necessary – with an appropriate Article 9 basis as well, of course.

3.7 The processing is necessary for reasons that can be demonstrated to be in the public interest

This is a broad category that has been developed in even greater detail under the Data Privacy Act 2018.

The starting point is Article 9(2)(g), which provides for lawful processing where the

> *processing is necessary for reasons of substantial public interest, on the basis of Union or Member State law which shall be proportionate to the aim pursued, respect the essence of the right to data protection and provide for suitable and specific measures to safeguard the fundamental rights and the interests of the Data Subject.*

Section 10(3) of the Data Protection Act 2018 establishes, for the UK, the relevant basis upon which a data processor may process special

"Journalism and the use of personal data is, naturally, a sensitive area and the ICO is required to produce a statutory code of practice to create a basis for compliance in this particular sector."

category data under Article 9(2)(g), with the detail set out in Schedule 1.[26] The subject matter is too extensive to deal with in detail here, but examples of the scope of these provisions include statutory and government purposes, equality of opportunity or treatment, journalism and academia, the arts and literature, and the prevention of fraud. A number of health-related reasons exist too, including support for individuals with disability or mental conditions, and counselling. Safeguarding of children at risk is another relevant area.

Journalism and the use of personal data is, naturally, a sensitive area and the ICO is required to produce a statutory code of practice to create a basis for compliance in this particular sector.[27]

3.8 Processing to provide medical or social care or treatment for particular conditions

Healthcare and social care are further important categories with their own sensitivities. Under Article 9(2)(h):

> *processing is necessary for the purposes of preventive or occupational medicine, for the assessment of the working capacity of the employee, medical diagnosis, the provision of health or social care or treatment or the management of health or social care systems and services on the basis of Union or Member State law or*

pursuant to contract with a health professional and subject to the conditions and safeguards referred to in paragraph 3.

Paragraph 3 referred to above (ie, Article 9(3)) sets an important precondition to the processing. The processing must be by or under the supervision of a professional who is subject to professional confidentiality obligations.

Article 9(2) covers processing of special category data in the following situations:

- preventive or occupational medicine;
- work assessments commissioned by an employer;
- for purposes of medical diagnosis;
- in order to provide healthcare or treatment;
- in order to provide social care (considered generally to include social work, personal care and social support services); and
- the management of healthcare systems or services or social care systems or services.

3.9 Processing is in the public interest for reasons of public health protection and the processing is necessary

This category has become a significant area of consideration, and even debate, as a consequence of the global COVID-19 pandemic. This easily transmitted disease has brought significant focus on the ability to track and trace transmission through communities affected.

Initiatives undertaken have also included emphasis on contact details for individuals visiting certain types of premises being required to provide contact information to the operators of the venue. A requirement to provide personal data runs against the concept of personal data being freely provided under the consent requirement; accordingly, legislative provisions have been put in place to formalise the legitimacy of the requirement in certain circumstances.

3.10 Processing of personal data on an archiving basis that is in the public interest or for purposes of scientific or historical research or on a statistical basis

A reminder, first, that data protection legislation relates only to living individuals.

The ability to process special category personal data is permitted where the processing is necessary for archiving purposes in the public interest, scientific or historical research purposes, or statistical purposes.

There is an important additional factor to take into account – Article

89(1) of the GDPR, which sets out requirements for technical or organisational measures to be in place to support compliance with the principle of data minimisation, in particular. In short, steps should be taken to consider the necessity of maintaining the status of the data as personal data, prior to the archiving taking place. Pseudonymisation should obviously be considered.

The reference to 'public interest' is notable – but if the UK continues to follow the EU GDPR, it is clear that the organisation pursuing the archiving activity can be within the private sector or indeed be a charity or other not-for-profit organisation.

A further point of importance can be found in Section 19 of the Data Protection Act 2018. The UK has developed the ground rules for special category data processing further by qualifying Article 89(1) of the GDPR to the effect that the article's requirements are not satisfied if the processing "is likely to cause substantial damage or substantial distress to a data subject".

Where the processing is carried out for the purpose of measures or decisions with respect to a particular data subject, Article 89(1) is further narrowed to require the particular processing to be associated with medical research and the conduct of the medical research must meet specific requirements found in Section 19(4) of the Data Protection Act, including a requirement that the processing be under the supervision of a medical professional.

4. What has happened to personal data relating to criminal offences and convictions?

The scope of special category data does not include matters of a criminal nature. This is in contrast with the previous position in the UK under the Data Protection Act 1998.

Criminal-related personal data is now treated separately. Article 6(1) of the GDPR states that:

> *[p]rocessing of personal data relating to criminal convictions for offences or related security measures based on article 6(1) shall be carried out only under the control of official authority or when the processing is organised by a union or member states law providing for appropriate safeguards rights and freedoms of Data Subjects. Any comprehensive register of convictions shall be kept only under the control of official authority.*

The mechanisms for control of such data are to be found in Part 3 of the Data Protection Act 2018. This part provides an extensive set of rules and requirements associated with the establishment of data as falling within the ambit of this category and the arrangements for processing of that data. The detail is not covered in this report.

However, given that personal data of this kind can initially be within the actual ambit of processing by data controllers not specifically tasked with criminal-related matters, the legislation needs to recognise this and does so. Examples would include capturing a shop-lifting incident on a supermarket's CCTV system and personal data held by an HR department that is likely to be evidential of the commitment of a criminal offence.

Processing in such cases is regarded in a similar way to that in which special category data is treated. Background checks undertaken appropriately by an employer are one example in which criminal data may be recorded.

VIII. Children's data – taking extra care

1. Introduction

A principle introduced by and developed further in the Data Protection Act 2018 is a greater recognition of the need to protect children where they provide their personal data.

Previous legislation had not sought to differentiate between children and adults. The past two decades have, however, witnessed an explosion of interactions that children have with technology, frequently involving sharing their personal data.

Many interest groups, including children's charities, argued that taking additional steps to recognise the needs and, in many cases, the potential vulnerability of young people was long overdue.

The context is set by Recital 38 of the EU GDPR, which recognises that children are entitled to special protection because they may be less aware of the risks, consequences and safeguards surrounding personal data.

A comparison with the US is interesting. While data protection laws there are generally left to each state to decide, a federal statute introduced in 1998 and known as the Children's Online Privacy Protection Act sets out standards of protection relating to children's data that has effect on a federal basis.

The key questions that will be seen to arise in the narrative below are:

- What is the legal definition of a 'child' for the purpose of data protection legislation?
- Are there considerations to be taken into account relating to privacy notices that children will access, be able to relate to and, through the detail contained within the notice, appreciate the implications of providing the requested information?
- How should consent be lawfully obtained from a child?
- Is it permissible to obtain data relating to children and then use that data for profiling purposes?
- What obligations should those who promote software and smartphone apps at consumer level have to make younger users aware of the consequences of use of the product and, importantly, the implications of privacy settings?
- If there are to be additional duties of care, how should differences in the level of maturity and comprehension of a child be taken into account? Should the publisher of the privacy notice be expected to address the notice to different levels of maturity and, if so, how can that be achieved in an effective manner?

"The GDPR does not require a service provider to establish the exact age of an individual but, rather, places a duty on the data controller to make sure that anyone giving their own consent is old enough to do so."

Another consideration is the lack of trusted and comprehensive age validation procedures: how will it be known for certain that a child is being truthful about his/her age?

The starting point for children's' data protection is Article 8(1) of the GDPR, which regulates the provision of information society services. The scope of such services is defined within EU legislation associated with e-commerce transactions and is surprisingly wide, covering all circumstances in which goods and services can be sold over the internet. Access to services of this kind in the UK by a person under the age of 13 should be permitted only with a parent's consent.[28]

2. How is a 'child' defined by age?

Reference was made to this subject above, but there is more to it in the overall make-up of data protection legislation. The EU GDPR delegated to individual member states the determination of a minimum age (ranging from 13 to 16) below which a consent could not be secured from a child. Member states may set their own age threshold. It is important to keep this in mind when services are offered to young persons in EU member states.

Under Section 9 of the Data Protection Act 2018, the UK determined that 13 was an appropriate age above which consent may be given by the individual.

This rule applies specifically to information society services; in other circumstances, there are no binding guidelines or statutory provisions to rely on. But 13 would seem in many respects to be appropriate as a more general rule.

The ICO notes that the GDPR does not require a service provider to establish the exact age of an individual but, rather, places a duty on the data controller to make sure that anyone giving their own consent is old enough to do so. Crucially, if this requirement is not successfully navigated the consent may not be relied upon as a lawful basis for processing. Unfortunately, there is no safe harbour provided by reference to any number of precautionary steps that a data controller may try to use prior to the consent being taken and acted upon.

What, then, must the data controller evidence in relation to obtaining consent from a child? When seeking to secure s child's consent, a data controller should:

> *make sure that the child understands what they are consenting to, and [does] not exploit any imbalance of power in the relationship between [the child and the Data Controller].*[29]

An important exemption from the requirement to ensure that an adult consent has been obtained, also within Section 9 of the Data Protection Act 2018, is in circumstances in which young people seek preventative or counselling services.

3. Privacy notices and children

When drafting privacy notices in relation to online products and services directed at children or where, even if that is not the case, children are nonetheless likely to seek and gain access, particular care is expected to be taken.[30] Effectively, in the context of children, compliance with the transparency principle requires the taking of additional steps when setting out the detail of personal data being collected and what happens to that data.

In its guidance the ICO draws attention to the fact that a data controller can raise children's (and their parents') awareness of data protection risks, consequences, safeguards and rights by:

- telling them what is being done with their personal data;
- being open about the risks and safeguards involved; and
- letting them know what to do if they are unhappy.

There is an expectation, in short, that the information provided through privacy notices addresses the audience appropriately, having regard to the age of the likely reader. Encouragement is given to simplified explanations, use of graphical illustrations and in overall terms – quite simply – a child-friendly and comprehensible approach to the exercise.

Key questions will always be:

- How should that consent be obtained?
- What is the data controller's position if it is difficult to determine the validity of any consent that is obtained?

Responsibility for monitoring compliance with the parental consent requirement rests with the data controller. Article 8(2) of the GDPR makes the controller responsible for securing the consent and limiting access where that consent is not available.

How far must a data controller go in establishing the validity of registrations to its site in age terms?

Much has been written on this subject. An attempt by the Department for Digital, Culture, Media and Sport some years ago to encourage the promotion of an age verification procedure for websites delivering adult content collapsed through the inability on the part of the

"Responsibility for monitoring compliance with the parental consent requirement rests with the data controller. Article 8(2) of the GDPR makes the controller responsible for securing the consent and limiting access where that consent is not available."

relevant industry to provide an effective solution. The challenge of verifying users' age remains a very real one.

4. Addressing differences in the maturity of children

Ensuring compliance when seeking to access and carry out other processing activities involving children's data requires attention to be paid to the following:

- The product or service that is intended to be made available, and which involves the processing of personal data, should have been designed in a way that includes consideration for the protection of the child and his/her data;
- If using a child's personal data for marketing purposes, particular considerations need to be taken into account by reason of the age of the target audience; and
- The way information is provided under the transparency duty requires particular consideration where children are involved. Providing information in a way that a child relates to is critical to compliance.

Recognising that the way that information is provided to a child should really reflect the age of a child and the maturity that will grow throughout the child's development has been a further area of significant debate. Age banding of information allowing a child to follow particular routes through privacy policies depending on age, for example, should be considered.

5. Other lawful bases – alternatives to consent?

The circumstances of any particular situation may provide a data controller with access to other lawful bases for processing the personal data of a child aside from consent. Other bases justifying the processing of the data include, for instance, legitimate interest, which by its nature requires looking at the balance of interests and thus creates the opportunity to take the age of the data subject specifically into account when considering whether the processing is permitted by law.

Frequently, the processing will be under the performance of tasks in the public interest and for reasons of protection of the vital interests of the child as the data subject.

6. Children and profiling

Where a product or service features in-built profiling that leads to particular decisions being taken relating to the child, the GDPR makes it clear that such profiling should usually not be undertaken on a purely automated basis.

7. Age-appropriate design

In a UK-specific addition to the protections afforded to children, the ICO has been required under the Data Protection Act 2018[31] to devise and publish an Age Appropriate Design Code of Practice (which the ICO is keen to promote as the 'Children's Code'). The definition of a child under the act provides 18 as the upper age limit, and the code requires developers and publishers affected to have regard to that particular age. The age-setting process and its outcome are based on a requirement made of the Information Commissioner that he/she take into account the UK's obligations under the United Nations Convention of the Rights of the Child.

Significantly, the Information Commissioner was also required to take into account the observation that children of different ages have different needs in the context of information to be provided concerning risks and how to address these.

This issue was exposed to debate and discussion during the consultation phase of the development of the Children's Code, which is discussed below.

While drafting the Data Protection Act 2018, the UK legislators decided to impose on developers and publishers of information society services the additional requirement to take particularly detailed steps to demonstrate that what is offered to the market satisfies the Children's Code when their services will be or are likely to be accessed by children (defined at that higher level of under 18 years).

The code builds on the principle of privacy by design and is generally taken to be unique, with no other country setting similar expectations of developers and publishers. Importantly, compliance with the code is expected where any service is made available within the UK, regardless of origin. The enforcement regime in relation to overseas organisations presents an interesting issue in its own right. Encouraging the ICO to take action in relation to any non-compliance may be the most obvious route to securing a court order requiring that internet service providers cease to make the service accessible. A test of that situation would be interesting, to say the least.

8. The requirements of the Age Appropriate Design Code

The GDPR requires that appropriate technical and organisational measures be put in place to implement the data protection principles and safeguard individual rights. This is 'data protection by design and by default'. This means that data protection must be integrated into

"Encouraging the ICO to take action in relation to any non-compliance may be the most obvious route to securing a court order requiring that internet service providers cease to make the service accessible. A test of that situation would be interesting, to say the least."

the processing activities and business practices, from the design stage right through the lifecycle.[32]

In a nutshell, this code is aimed at establishing standards for the design of the privacy-related features of a service. The breadth of applications of the code should be understood. It is regarded as covering all of the following:

- apps;
- programs;
- connected toys and other devices;
- search engines;
- social media platforms;
- streaming services;
- online games;
- news and educational websites; and
- websites offering goods and services for sale over the internet.

The remit of the ICO is, of course, entirely associated with the protection of personal data and the code is suitably limited in scope. The focus is appropriate safeguarding of children's personal data.

"There are no fewer than 15 standards (not all applicable in each individual case) that developers and publishers will need to take into account throughout the development phase of a product – with these also now being addressed retrospectively if necessary."

The code sets out specific protections that services offered should be expected to satisfy and have been built in during the development of the service. There is however no saving regime for services already fully developed – to address that issue, a transitional period of a year ending on 2 September 2021 has been provided to allow reference back to design and development teams to do further privacy-related work if necessary.

The code sets out practical measures and safeguards to ensure that processing is fair in the context of online risks to children. An early criticism of the code has been that while these measures and safeguards are described as 'standards', the ability to assess compliance against a number of these is not straightforward.

The requirements are made of all relevant organisations, including charities and voluntary bodies. The ICO Regulatory Action Policy[33] will apply to enforcement.

There are no fewer than 15 standards (not all applicable in each individual case) that developers and publishers will need to take into account throughout the development phase of a product – with these also now being addressed retrospectively if necessary.

The 15 standards are:

- best interests of the child demonstrated;
- data protection impact assessment appropriately worked through;
- age-appropriate application;
- transparency;
- detrimental use of data;
- policies and community standards;
- default setting;
- data minimisation;
- data sharing;
- geolocation;
- parental controls;
- profiling;
- nudge techniques;
- connected toys and devices; and
- online tools.

An initial task that will usually be appropriate is to develop and complete a data protection impact assessment. Chapter 2 of the code addresses this requirement and introduces the subject in the following way:

> *Undertake a DPIA [data protection impact assessment] to assess and mitigate risks to the rights and freedoms of children who are likely to access your service, which arise from your data processing. Take into account differing ages, capacities and development needs and ensure that your DPIA builds in compliance with this code.*

Guidance within the code points developers and publishers to ensuring that the operational characteristics of products and services available to children feature:

- privacy settings at their most private by default;
- behavioural-based advertising also switched off by default;
- data sharing at the lowest level provided by default; and
- user location switched off by default.

It is also an expectation that attempts to change default settings should be blocked in areas of functionality such as behavioural-based advertising.

There is a particular challenge where an app or web-based service is legitimately accessed by both children and adults. In such cases, should there be any difficulty in taking into account the age of a child and presenting a child user with pre-determined lowest level settings, then the ICO's position is that relevant standards in the code should be applied to all users.

IX. Managing photographs and video personal data

1. Introduction

Photographs, videos and other media in digital format constitute personal data. Photographs can also form part of the personal data held in hard copy documents – for example, a photograph of a person affixed to a hard copy CV.

The issue of video recording (in the form of CCTV) is also an area requiring compliance. Importantly, it is an aspect of data protection law in which the domestic activities of an individual (which would usually fall outside of data protection regulation) can become subject to data protection legislation as we shall see.

Straight away, we can draw parameters around this issue and note that taking photographs or videos on a social basis generally falls outside of legislative control. Restrictions might arise in other ways, such as when child protection and security considerations are taken into account – taking photographs at school events is frequently discouraged and invitations to visit stately homes can require restraint in the use of photography. But any photographs or videos captured can be freely shared, uploaded to Facebook and other social media platforms without steps being taken to obtain any consents.

It might be thought that uploading material to Facebook brings the photograph or video concerned within the parameters of data protection legislation – and it does, in the sense that data subject rights apply to a certain extent. But Facebook does not become the data controller for media and is processing the personal data provided not under documented instructions in the manner required by the GDPR, since there is no data controller.

There are, however, circumstances in which a photograph or video taken in a social context finds its way into the regulated environment of an organisation. The relative ease with which one can re-tweet and forward other social media-based material means that, on occasions, media that originated in an uncontrolled manner falls into control.

Case study

When personal photographs become personal data

A primary school hosts a sports day attended by parents. Photographs taken by parents find their way onto Instagram and Facebook. The primary school has its own accounts with these social media platforms. Photographs are re-tweeted by a member of staff with additional comments – perhaps congratulations to the race winner. The school is very likely to be regarded as a data controller acting as such in these circumstances, since it will have editing rights to the material that is republished. The case is even stronger – indeed, conclusive – if the photographs are saved onto the school's server to use, for example, in further school-initiated publicity.

2. How should an organisation relate compliance to photographs and videos taken within the organisation?

Advances in technology have made for a multitude of scenarios in which personal data is captured, usually with the data subject's knowledge, but often without. Examples of personal data capture that we can consider include:

- CCTV recordings in shopping malls, hotels, the workplace and schools;
- recording of Zoom or Teams calls within the work place;
- video taken at events by news media showing bystanders and audience members;
- vehicle number plate detection systems on highways and motorways; and
- facial recognition-based policing systems.

When working through compliance requirements, the starting point will always be to consider what the nature of the personal data captured is which falls into the category of photography, video or other media. As with documented data, it is all down to just what data

"Advances in technology have made for a multitude of scenarios in which personal data is captured, usually with the data subject's knowledge, but often without."

is held by the organisation. In this chapter, we are looking at the position of an organisation as data controller – processing compliance for the data controller will be no different to the position with other forms of personal data.

The next step is to consider the circumstances: why is the data being captured and then processed? Is the capture in all cases intended or is some of that incidental? For instance, CCTV cameras mounted at the entry point to a shop may capture passers-by. Keeping in mind the data minimisation requirement, a point that will need consideration is the location of the camera and whether the location is optimal in terms of capturing data that is relevant to the purpose versus data that is incidental. A poorly located camera within a school playground that captures imagery of a neighbour's garden would be an example of a situation to be avoided.

How the data controller then carries forward its process of considering compliance requirements will depend on the circumstances. Let us look in detail at two examples that provide a useful overview of many compliance issues:

- staff imagery used for security and other business purposes; and
- CCTV recording.

3. Staff imagery

Photographs of staff tend to be used in two specific circumstances:

- for security purposes linked to a mandatory requirement to wear ID when present on the organisation's premises and often when representing the organisation at external meetings or to confirm authorisation to a person being visited; and
- for business development purposes – presenting details of staff members on a website and in published brochures.

To take advantage of the use of photography in these circumstances will require consideration of the lawful basis upon which the photographs are being used. For security purposes, the legitimate interest of the organisation will be most relevant. One should keep in mind – as explained in Chapter IV – that basing data processing on consent in an employer/employee relationship is not considered best practice. So it is helpful to be able to call upon legitimate interest. Where the photograph is taken for security purposes, the balancing of the interests required is likely to be straightforward.

Likewise, the use of a photograph taken to support the marketing activities of the business will most likely be considered an application of the legitimate interests of the employer. The employee concerned should, as a matter of best practice, have the right to be aware of the likely use and, in the vast majority of cases, will have no issue – particularly if the intended result is to promote the reputation of the individual as an employee of the organisation.

The issue of informing the individual of an intended or possible use of photographs is, of course, also addressed through the fair processing notice provided to staff members which should reflect this particular activity.

As with other personal data, the data subject has the right to require that the organisation delete and/or restrict the processing of the imagery held. It is prudent to address this right through staff policies and the employment contract, by making an appropriate reference to the data subject's right but also highlighting the consequences of both deletion and processing restriction – for example, with regard to access to the organisation's premises and therefore the individual's ability to actually perform his or her role.

4. CCTV recording

The wide availability of CCTV recording technology makes it a straightforward matter for an organisation to invest in the technology. In addition, there has been a very significant growth in offerings of this kind available for domestic security purposes.

The ICO makes its compliance expectations in this regard clear through a dedicated CCTV information page. There is particular emphasis on data minimisation, making the location of the CCTV cameras and the field of image capture a critical consideration. The ICO strongly advises against placing cameras in an outward facing position as this has the potential to capture images of individuals present on adjoining properties; the ICO also stresses the additional compliance responsibilities that would arise in consequence of such a practice.

Where imagery is captured of individuals beyond the property of the system owner, data protection compliance requirements must be observed. Importantly, the legislation is also applicable to domestic uses of systems in such circumstances. Registration with the ICO is not required, but the ICO can investigate the use and take action where complaints are made.

The ICO's recommended approach, which should be taken into account prior to CCTV being implemented, involves the following considerations:

- Is a CCTV system really necessary?
- Has the system been set up in the most privacy-friendly manner?
- Is recording the images captured necessary?
- If the system has audio recording, has that function been disabled?

Crucially, the practice of capturing imagery outside of the premises occupied brings the user into scope as a data controller. In consequence, the formal requirements to respond to data subject access requests and other data subject rights come into play.

X. Information governance – what the law expects

1. What is meant by accountability?

A reference was made to accountability among the key principles set out in Chapter III. The accountability principle requires serious consideration: it is not just about having rules and systems in place to ensure that an organisation is complying with the law; it is also about being able to provide evidence of that compliance.

Accountability starts with the assessment by an organisation of the risks that exist associated with the processing of personal data within that organisation, by those that are subcontracted to undertake processing activities on behalf of the data controller and, also, around decisions taken that lead to personal data being shared with third parties.

The assessment must have tangible outcomes – namely, as mentioned above, to be able to demonstrate compliance with the law.

2. How to demonstrate accountability

The ICO provides some helpful suggestions within its Accountability Framework.[34] At the time of writing, this has been published in draft form for the purposes of a consultation. The most significant benefit likely to be derived from taking the framework into account when reviewing accountability within an organisation is the breakdown of the duty into a number of risk areas. These are:

- leadership and oversight;
- policies and procedures;
- training and awareness;
- individual rights;
- contracts and data sharing;
- risks and data protection impact assessment;
- records management and security; and
- breach response and monitoring.

When considering whether an organisation demonstrates strong accountability, the starting point will always be the governance arrangements that are implemented within the organisation. The following will be regarded as the required tangible evidence of that standard of governance:

- The organisation has established oversight at the highest level of the organisation's management structure – this will usually be a board and, ideally, an individual within the board is tasked to be the lead in data protection. This could be particularly important as that person becomes the 'go to' person for the data protection officer (DPO), where that position exists;
- Management lead by example in their demonstration of the

"When considering whether an organisation demonstrates strong accountability, the starting point will always be the governance arrangements that are implemented within the organisation."

significance to the organisation of the management of risks relating to data protection;
- There are clear reporting lines and the lines of communication are effective – in particular, those who are responsible for information governance and who manage aspects of data protection are empowered to fulfil their roles and responsibilities; and
- Policies are in place and job descriptions are written such that responsibilities for various aspects of data protection compliance can be clearly understood by those who carry these responsibilities and by others who work with key individuals.

Case study

Doorstep dispensaree

This was the very first case determined by the ICO under the GDPR and involved fining an organisation that was found not to have appropriate technical and organisational measures in place to support the security of personal data held. The ICO imposed a fine of £275,000.[35]

The case involved a dispensing chemist that chose to store a filing cabinet containing prescription documentation for patients outside a back door to the pharmacy – exposed to the elements and therefore risking theft and deterioration in the integrity of the personal data. No actual loss of data had been reported, so this is a helpful representation of how the accountability duty must be capable of being demonstrated and failures penalised by the ICO, even when there is no actual compromise to personal data.

3. When is a DPO required?

Organisations acting as data controllers or data processors must, under the GDPR, consider whether it is necessary to appoint a DPO. In certain cases, it is mandatory to identify and appoint a DPO as will be explained below.

It is permissible to appoint a DPO when this is not mandatory. In practice, there are two possible scenarios that need to be considered and it is important that the organisation indeed considers both. These are:

- where, having assessed the circumstances of the organisation and if the criteria that apply under the GDPR make it necessary to appoint a DPO, the organisation must proceed to do so; and
- where, even if the circumstances of the organisation do not require an appointment, there may be particular risk factors that the organisation is keen to recognise, in which case a decision can be taken to appoint a DPO on a voluntary basis.

4. When is it mandatory to appoint a DPO?
Public authorities must appoint a DPO. This should be taken to extend to private sector organisations that are performing public services, if the view taken by the European Data Protection Board is followed.[36] Perhaps controversially, the view taken by the board in the case of private sector organisations is that if there is a requirement to appoint a DPO, his/her duties should extend to all data protection compliance requirements of the organisation – even those that go beyond the performance of public sector functions. It is not known whether post-Brexit the UK courts will be minded to take the same approach.

The requirement to appoint a DPO in the case of every public body does create a dilemma for smaller legally constituted public bodies. To give an example, governing bodies of schools are regarded by the ICO as the responsible party for schools' data protection compliance, meaning that even the smallest of primary schools may be duty bound to make an appointment.

To address that kind of issue, the GDPR permits any organisation (public or private) to outsource the role, as will be explained below.

5. When is a private sector organisation required to appoint a DPO?
The requirement focuses on circumstances where the 'core activities' of the organisation involve:

- regular and systematic monitoring of data subjects on a large scale; and/or
- processing on a large scale of special category data or personal data relating to criminal convictions and offences within the scope of Article 10 of the GDPR.

The core activities of an organisation need to be considered as functions carried out to which the processing of personal data forms an integral part. By way of example, the operation by a major retailer of a loyalty card that, when used, records the detail of products purchased would clearly fall within the scope of this requirement.

6. What are the implications of making a voluntary appointment?
A decision to identify an individual as DPO may still be regarded as prudent, even when the criteria requiring an appointment are not met. But the implications of doing so need to be understood.

As a starting point, the formalities associated with such an appointment need to be followed and the existence of a DPO made clear within privacy notices published by the organisation, as well as by notification to the ICO. It is worth noting (and this applies to all DPO appointments) that the identity of the individual appointed does not require to be recorded in a privacy notice – the use of contact details in the form of, for example, 'DPO@ourorg.co.uk' is acceptable.

A DPO appointed on a voluntary basis will have the same duties as a DPO appointed on a mandatory basis, although the UK GDPR does not (and neither did the EU GDPR) provide for employment protection in such circumstances.

7. Deciding not to appoint a DPO – make sure the decision is recorded in writing!

Undoubtedly one of the most overlooked points of detail within the GDPR is the expectation that a decision not to appoint a DPO should be recorded in writing with the reasons for that decision forming part of the record. Many organisations will have unwittingly flouted this requirement. When considering accountability of the organisation, the ICO may ask to see such a record. However, given the far more significant issues that may be under review by the ICO (possibly even whether the decision not to appoint was, in fact, correct), this is unlikely to ever be seen as a material failing.

"A DPO appointed on a voluntary basis will have the same duties as a DPO appointed on a mandatory basis, although the UK GDPR does not (and neither did the EU GDPR) provide for employment protection in such circumstances."

"Questions to answer [in relation to the adequate resourcing of a DPO within an organisation] are: Should there be staff specifically supporting the DPO? Is there a budget for external legal advice? Does the DPO have sufficient time available for the task to be performed effectively?"

8. What are the duties of a DPO?

The duties are to be found in Article 37 of the GDPR. It may be helpful here to refer to a paper produced by the Article 29 Working Party[37] that provided further guidance in relation to the way the duties should be performed. While the UK has not adopted the EU guidance, this publication provides at the very least an indication of what may be considered to be good practice.

When writing a DPO job description, the following should be considered (regardless of whether the role is internally resourced or outsourced to an expert provider):

- Accessibility – regarded as a point of reference for internal staff, but also third parties such as data subjects.
- Adequate resourcing – specific consideration should be given in the context of the data protection risks that are to be managed within the organisation as to the extent of resourcing. Questions to answer are: Should there be staff specifically supporting the DPO? Is there a budget for external legal advice? Does the DPO have sufficient time available for the task to be performed effectively (since the role is not necessarily full time)?
- Demonstration of skills and expertise – the DPO must be able to demonstrate an understanding of the role and the ability to perform it with competence.
- Involvement in the affairs of the organisation – possibly one of the trickiest areas will be to develop a culture and to ensure practical arrangements around the quasi-independence of the DPO, while also ensuring that the DPO is appropriately engaged in the business and affairs of the organisation. By way of example, keeping a DPO at a distance from a project would not be regarded as a sound working practice, particularly if the project requires a data protection impact assessment – something that must be developed in parallel with the life of the project, as shall be seen later in this chapter. The DPO must be kept alive to the risks the organisation has associated with the management of personal data at all times.
- Alongside involvement, the ability to act and think independently – the monitoring role played is such that the DPO must not be subject to being influenced or lobbied around decisions (sometimes difficult) that require to be taken.
- Security of tenure – while usual employment law considerations apply and the tenure of the DPO, if an employee, can be subject to usual disciplinary procedures (poor performance in that role must, obviously, be capable of being dealt with), the DPO cannot be disciplined for legitimately and correctly performing his/her role (Article 38(3) of the GDPR).

- Conflict of interest – a further difficult issue for many organisations is the requirement to separate the role of DPO from individuals performing other roles and with whom the DPO could come into conflict. A chief executive officer would not be regarded as an appropriate individual to be appointed given his/her oversight responsibility for the entire organisation. As the quality of technological security in the organisation could be brought into question by the DPO, the chief technical officer is also to be considered disbarred from acting as DPO. Even the chief financial officer is regarded as having a potential conflict of interest due to the attitude that could be taken to the possible financial consequences of a data breach incident and the role that person would play in managing the financial resources available to the DPO.

9. Outsourcing the DPO role

It is perhaps surprising, given the significance of the role of DPO, that organisations are entitled to outsource the role to a third party – either an individual or an organisation. Article 37(6) of the GDPR provides for this. There are no pre-conditions to outsourcing and the existence of this ability is of great importance to smaller organisations where the practicalities of performing the function in-house is

"It is perhaps surprising, given the significance of the role of DPO, that organisations are entitled to outsource the role to a third party – either an individual or an organisation."

challenging – given, in particular, the requirement to create a degree of independence in the role and the importance of avoiding conflict of interest.

Outsourcing the role does not, however, absolve the organisation appointing from any of the duties and, therefore, the financial responsibilities relating to performing the role of data controller or data processor. The appointment therefore requires particular due diligence, ensuring also that the service provider holds appropriate insurances and is an appropriate party to be granted access to the personal data that the appointment relates to.

10. Record keeping

Whether or not an organisation has a DPO, record keeping is an important task in both the demonstration of compliance through accountability and, quite simply, to make life easier when issues arise such as data breaches and data subject access requests.

The GDPR provides a number of duties to be complied with in relation to record keeping. The requirements support the accountability and transparency duties in particular.

There are a number of specific records to be maintained – the requirements are, however, modified for smaller organisations (those with fewer than 250 employees).

In more detail, the record keeping requirements relate to both data controllers and data processors.

In the case of a data controller, the requirements cover:

- the name and contact details for the data controller including, where relevant, details of the DPO;
- the purposes for which processing is undertaken;
- details of data subjects by category and the categories of personal data processed;
- activities involving transfers of personal data to third countries or to international organisations;
- time limits for erasure of the various categories of personal data where it is possible to declare this; and
- a general description of the technical and organisational measures in place to protect personal data.

In the case of a data processor, the requirements cover:

- the name and contact details for the data processor and information relating to data controllers whose data is processed

  by the data processor and including, where relevant, details of the DPO;
- categories of processing carried out for each data controller;
- activities involving transfers of personal data to third countries or to international organisations; and
- a general description of the technical and organisational measures in place to protect personal data.

The ICO is entitled to require production of the records on request.

Article 30(5) of the GDPR provides exemptions for small employers, unless the processing undertaken is likely to result in a risk to the rights and freedoms of data subjects, the processing is not occasional, or the processing specifically involves special category data or data relating to criminal convictions or offences.

11. Data protection impact assessments – what are they?
Article 35 of the GDPR formalises what is considered to be, in data protection terms, an important practice, known as data protection impact assessments. The purpose of an assessment is to establish, evaluate and manage risks. For a number of years, the ICO promoted as best practice the adoption of such assessments when data controllers or data processors were developing new ways of processing personal data. This has now become a legislative requirement in appropriate circumstances following the implementation of the EU GDPR.

Article 35(1) sets the scene as follows:

> *Where a type of processing in particular using new technologies, and taking into account the nature, scope, context and purposes of the processing, is likely to result in a high risk to the rights and freedoms of natural persons, the controller shall, prior to the processing, carry out an assessment of the impact of the envisaged processing operations on the protection of personal data.*

So, when undertaking new projects or making serious changes to the way any personal data is stored or used within an organisation, a data protection impact assessment becomes a mandatory tool as part of a risk management process.

Data protection impact assessments must be conducted by law when any data processing that an organisation intends to undertake is likely to result in a high risk for the individuals whose data is processed. Specifically, an assessment is mandatory when:

- processing involves using data for profiling purposes or to make

big decisions about individuals automatically using the data processed;
- special category or criminal offence data is to be processed on a large scale;
- the organisation intends to adopt innovative technology (eg, commissioning an artificial intelligence-powered process) that is likely to have an effect on individuals;
- a project involves implementation of a system processing biometric or genetic data; or
- processing is intended to track individuals' online or offline location.

Conducting an assessment is encouraged in a range of other circumstances, such as when children's personal data is to be processed, systematic monitoring of data subjects is proposed, new technology is being adopted and where processing could involve preventing data subjects from exercising a particular right or using a particular service.

The key point to have in mind when thinking about data protection impact assessments is risk. Risks exist in any organisation, in all sorts of ways. For many organisations, risks relating to personal data will

"Data protection impact assessments must be conducted by law when any data processing that an organisation intends to undertake is likely to result in a high risk for the individuals whose data is processed."

be minimal – think of a market stall selling fresh produce with cash or automated transactions where the vendor has no practical access to the customer's data as it is transacted.

By contrast, think then about a fast-growing brick-and-mortar business that is moving its business online having already amassed hundreds of customers.

For that latter business, risk in relation to personal data is likely to be significant and serious time and resources should be dedicated to matters of compliance – this will be expected of that business under the accountability duty.

Staying with this example, the business currently operates in a very basic way. It has a retail shop that it proposes to close as online orders are increasing. As part of the closure process, considerable emphasis is placed on collecting contact details from customers – information is requested and recorded on paper forms that will in due course be inputted to a cloud-based customer relations management (CRM) system that the owners have just taken out a subscription to.

Information is then transcribed manually from the forms into an online database suitable for use in both the management of marketing mail shots and sales transactions. A small sales team has also been hired to handle telephone marketing and telephone sales to complement online sales through the business's website.

This case study is given in this level of detail to emphasise that:

- already, the business has implemented what might seem a surprisingly large number of activities that bring data protection compliance considerations into play; and
- the business may already be in breach of data protection requirements expected of it and will lack the ability to demonstrate to the ICO that it is taking sufficient steps to demonstrate its accountability for the personal data that it has collected and is now expected to be managing in a compliant way.

To demonstrate the role played by a data protection impact assessment, let's take a look at all that has happened with this business so far and what risks may become embedded in the business and result in data protection compliance breaches.

Table 5. How personal data is impacted and the resultant risks

The task	How personal data is impacted	What risks arise?
The business starts to take records of customers' personal data.	Customers will, in the vast majority of cases, willingly provide the information requested. But have they been told how it will be used and does the form to be completed provide sufficient detail to the customers for this to become an informed consent? Have the customers been offered the option to refuse marketing mailshots – and if so, why is the information still being collected?	From the outset, the business meets compliance issues – the compilation of a paper-based file of customer information meets the definition of a 'structured database', meaning that the data collected falls under data protection legislation. A privacy notice should be provided and made available for the customers to review before the data is collected. And the data subjects must be made aware that the personal data is being collected for database purposes – not just in connection with a sale transaction just being completed. There is the possibility that the collation of the information is not organised securely, with individual forms possibly mislaid or even left visible on the shop counter.
The business must take the step of registering as a data controller with the ICO, paying the necessary annual fee.	No direct impact.	Non-compliance with the registration duty leaves the business open to a fine.

continued on next page

The task	How personal data is impacted	What risks arise?
The documented customer information is then manually transcribed into a CRM cloud service.	Manual transcription can lead to errors, with the resulting data set for a particular customer not being accurate. The data is also immediately passing into the hands of a data processor which is contracted to hold and make available the data as instructed by the business.	If the business fails to undertake appropriate due diligence with regard to the service provider that it has contracted, the data may later be found to have been processed by a party located in a third country without data protection laws that assure adequate protection of the personal data.
The sales team then springs into action and starts a tele-sales campaign to advise customers that the online business is now up and running.	The team lacks training in how to undertake their role and the responsibilities they have to support the business in its data protection compliance. In addition, the CRM system is not sufficient to safeguard information – essentially, a well-developed system should employ gates blocking access to data until actually required to speak to a specific customer.	The lack of appropriate training exposes the business to risk in relation to personal data breaches. The business may not have considered fully the implications of providing full access to a customer database to members of staff who could subsequently leave the business taking a copy of the data for use in a new employment elsewhere.

The above is far from comprehensive of the issues and the risks that can arise, but the example serves to demonstrate that it is reasonable for the legislation to require a carefully considered and planned approach to developing a new business model – or, indeed, making significant changes to an existing way of doing business.

12. How to undertake a data protection impact assessment

A data protection impact assessment is the process of assessing and considering risks that may arise from a particular project that is being embarked on. The assessment should be documented. The ICO expects an assessment to:

- describe the nature, scope, context and purposes of the processing that will occur;
- assess the necessity, proportionality and compliance measures associated with the processing;

- identify and assess risks to individuals; and
- identify and record a risk management strategy.[38]

13. Tools to keep an organisation on the straight and narrow

For larger organisations, a key tool is likely to be a form of operations manual that provides a framework under which data protection compliance is managed. The framework should focus on:

- individuals' roles and responsibilities;
- reporting procedures – particularly to the board or governing body of the organisation;
- procedures related to induction of new personnel and periodic staff training;
- a detailed statement of the personal data collected and processed by the organisation – ideally identifying ownership of particular data sets being linked to particular key roles;
- procedures when data is about to be shared or processed by a third party;
- staff policies related to data protection issues;
- other policies, such as that for the system of data retention, procedures for responding to data subject access requests and social media use within the organisation; and
- an overview of the technical measures that the business has in place to protect and provide appropriate levels of access to personal data and how cybercrime and other technical risks are managed.

14. And don't forget the responsibility to keep up to date

This responsibility involves:

- taking account of developments in the legislation and update both procedures and documentation in response;
- making sure that any change in the allocation of data protection-related responsibilities is implemented when there are personnel changes; and
- updating privacy notices, internal rules and procedures when making any change to processing activities involving personal data, as well as considering whether there will now be a need either for a data protection impact assessment or to revisit an existing assessment associated with the data processing involved.

Case study

Limiting access to personal data

An accountancy practice specialises in managing the tax affairs of professional footballers. It therefore holds particularly sensitive data associated with high-profile individuals. The data is ring-fenced to ensure that only particular individuals may access it. Such ring-fencing would be an example of the business taking an extra step to manage the data. While this step may seem to give the message that the business does not trust unauthorised staff, it is exactly how that business can demonstrate compliance.

15. Responding to data breaches

What, exactly, constitutes a data breach?

Article 4(12) of the GDPR defines it as:

> *a breach of security leading to the accidental or unlawful destruction, loss, alteration, unauthorised disclosure of, or access to, personal data transmitted, stored or otherwise processed.*

Therefore, a number of different situations amount to a data breach and the scope is far from limited to cyber-security situations where systems are penetrated and data extracted in circumstances that are manifestly criminal. The range of circumstances in which a data breach might occur is wide. Examples would include:

- shoulder surfing (ie, looking over the shoulder of) an employee carrying out work on a train (thus gaining access to personal data);
- the loss of a USB stick containing personal data;
- data lost when an organisation is attempting to transition to a new computer system involving the migration of the data across to the new system; and
- loss of a password making it impossible to access the data.

Not all breaches will require a response in the form of notification to the ICO and the data subject, but the circumstances and the implications of the breach will need to be assessed by reference to the reporting requirements of the GDPR set out in Article 33.

The question to be addressed (applying Article 33) is as follows: Is the data breach likely to result in a risk to the rights and freedoms of natural persons? Where the data breach concerns, for instance, banking details or health-related data, the answer is most likely easy to determine. There will be nuances around more benign data, meaning that each case needs to be carefully assessed and a determination made whether to notify the ICO or not.

"The scope [of a data breach] is far from limited to cyber-security situations where systems are penetrated and data extracted in circumstances that are manifestly criminal."

That determination needs to be made swiftly. A notification is expected to be made to the ICO within 72 hours of becoming aware of the data breach. Weekends and public holidays are counted in this calculation.

The responsibility rests with the data controller, which presents a particular challenge where personal data has been entrusted to a third-party data processor and the breach occurs at that level: the data controller must be notified of the breach in the first place so that an assessment and decision to report can be made, where appropriate. A contractual duty imposed on the data processor is all that a data controller can implement in an effort to comply with its reporting duty.

Article 33(3) sets out very specific requirements for a breach notification to be compliant – namely, the notification must:

- outline the nature of the breach and categories (with numbers) of data subjects affected, together with details of the data records involved;
- provide the contact details of the DPO or other source of the information;
- explain the likely consequences of the breach; and
- provide the details of measures taken and proposed to be taken to mitigate the possible adverse effects of the data breach.

It may not be feasible to provide full information at the time of the notification and the notification can be supplemented with further information later, but always in a way that does not demonstrate undue delay.

As a general rule, in accordance with Article 34(3) the need to notify the ICO is likely to mean that affected data subjects should also be notified of the breach. This is, however, a separate decision to be made. In making its decision, the data controller is entitled to consider three circumstances in which a notification need not be made. These are:

- notwithstanding the fact that the personal data may have ended up in a third party's hands, the technical and organisational measures implemented by the relevant party make the data unintelligible with the result that no use can be made of it (eg, the data is encrypted);
- particular steps taken have eliminated any high risk to the individual notwithstanding the occurrence of the data breach; and
- notification would involve disproportionate effort. In this case the use of some form of public communication would be expected, rather than the data controller taking no action at all.

The communication to the data subject should provide the same information as that used in the notification to the ICO.

Data controllers and data processors must maintain a log of the data breach, the effect of the breach and steps taken following the breach – the ICO being entitled to require access to the log for inspection purposes.

XI. Managing subject access rights

1. Introduction

The GDPR presents data controllers with a responsibility to provide an individual with access to data held concerning that individual. The individual's rights, however, extend significantly beyond the best-known rule – namely, that a copy of all data that a data subject is entitled to and has requested be provided within one calendar month of the date of request (importantly, the request can be oral).

In summary, the rights of the data subject are:

- a right to be informed about processing that will be undertaken (this aspect is addressed in Chapter VI);
- a right to access personal data held;
- a right to have personal data which is not accurate corrected or updated;
- a right to have personal data deleted;
- a right to require restriction of the data controller's data processing;
- a right to data portability – enabling transfers of data to an alternative service provider; and
- rights related to automated decision making (this aspect is addressed in Chapter XIII).

2. Let's call these the data subject access responsibilities
It is immediately apparent that the data subject access responsibilities present a number of challenges to the data controller. The starting point for the data controller in responding to the requirements to meet requests from data subjects is clearly to have a strong information management structure in place. When the accountability duty (explained in Chapter X) is also taken into account, the responsibility is an even deeper one – requiring the data controller to be able to demonstrate that it can meet the subject access responsibilities through the data governance procedures that it has in place.

Taking each of the rights not covered elsewhere in this report in turn, the following are important considerations for the data controller.

3. Meeting the right of access to personal data
This is by far the best-known right among data subjects, with its use applied in many different circumstances ranging from an individual anxious to understand the extent and detail of the data held, to individuals pursuing, for example, litigation or employment tribunal proceedings. There is no need for the data subject to provide any reason or justification for making a request (more on this below). Where an individual is tempted, however, to make multiple requests, a legislative brake exists to assist the data controller in managing the situation, as explained below.

As mentioned in section 1 above, there is no requirement for the data subject to make the request in writing – a conversation between a patient and a receptionist at a health centre during which the patient makes a request for personal data to be provided is enough to trigger the subject access procedures – meaning that careful training of staff and the efficient translation of the request into a process that the data controller then embarks on is of great importance.

Article 15 of the GDPR provides that the data subject may request to know, in addition to detail that has been provided or ought to have been provided in a privacy notice, the following:

- details of the personal data held (a copy of the personal data held must be provided in response to the request, unless an exception applies);
- how that personal data is being processed by, or for, the data controller;
- who the personal data is shared with; and
- where the personal data was obtained from.

In the early days of data protection law, many made the assumption that requesting access to personal data was in order to check the data's accuracy and to have certainty that it was being processed lawfully. Data controllers are free to restrict access to legally privileged information and must take care not to disclose personal data concerning individuals unconnected with the request. But is there a broader right to refuse access if the purpose is to pursue some claim or case against the data controller unconnected with data protection legislation?

A series of court cases arose in which requests had been made, but where the relationship between the data controller and the data subject involved litigation in some form or other and where the data controller believed that the purpose of requesting access was predominantly for the purposes of the litigation. Was that a fair use of the data subject access right?

In *Dawson Damer v Taylor Wessing LLP*,[39] the Court of Appeal observed, through Lord Justice Auld, that the concept of there being a need to demonstrate that there was no other purpose for a data subject access request than merely checking the data's accuracy and validity of processing represented a misunderstanding of the position.

"Data controllers are free to restrict access to legally privileged information and must take care not to disclose personal data concerning individuals unconnected with the request."

A further consideration in terms of planning to deal compliantly with data subject access requests is the one-month period within which the request must be responded to and the personal data provided. This may seem a straightforward and reasonably long period. Many organisations, though, will hold data in a number of locations, making it time consuming to retrieve. The response will also need to reflect non-digital data held – documents may need to be located.

Where the request is complex, the data controller can require a further period of up to two months to deliver its response to the data subject's request, provided that the data subject is notified of the need for additional time during the initial one-month period.

In order to be able to respond within the required time period and (to the advantage of the organisation) in the most resource-efficient way, an organisation will need to have developed strong information management procedures and good documentation of locations where data sits. As noted in Chapter X, employers with more than 250 employees and certain others are required to maintain registers of personal data held. This will put any organisation (whether it does so as a compliance measure or on a voluntary basis) in an excellent position to respond to a data subject access request.

The response must be provided free of charge, unless it represents a duplication of a response previously made or where the request is considered "manifestly unfounded or excessive"[40] – an expression that is, unfortunately, not defined. The ICO attempts to provide guidance, suggesting that the following considerations are relevant:

- The request is made with no real purpose except to cause harassment or disruption;
- The motivations of the data subject expressed to the data controller make the request inappropriate; and
- There is an overlap with a request that has yet to be responded to – meaning that the data subject should await the first response before making a further request.

Where it is appropriate to regard the request as manifestly unfounded or excessive, the requestor can be advised of a refusal to respond or may be charged an appropriate amount for the information to be provided.

4. Exclusions to the requirement to respond

This complex area needs to be navigated carefully. At a minimum, the data subject must be told which exemption is being relied upon, with justifications given, and how the decision to claim exemption can be challenged.

"Responding to a data subject access request too quickly could be a mistake and actually lead to a personal data breach."

Detailed guidance on exemptions is provided on the ICO website.[41] Any organisation concerned about the sensitivity of information and having taken a view that it may wish not to respond – indeed, might not even be entitled to respond (eg, in the area of potential money laundering) – should consult the guidance and act accordingly.

5. Preparing to make a response

Responding to a data subject access request too quickly could be a mistake and actually lead to a personal data breach or other forms of non-compliance with legal requirements.

When a request is made, the responding organisation is required to satisfy itself that the request is being made by the data subject or by a person with satisfactory authority to make the request on behalf of the data subject. Judgement is required by reference to the particular circumstances – a request from an employee presents little difficulty in identity verification, whereas a request by email from a patient addressed to a health centre that has not dealt with that individual by email previously would require additional identity verification.

A second issue to address before responding is whether the individual making the request is entitled to the information requested. A series of restrictions provided under the GDPR (further developed in the

Data Protection Act 2018)[42] needs to be considered. The restrictions cover:

- matters of national security;
- protection of UK defences;
- issues involving investigation of criminal activity broadened out to also reflect risk to public security;
- where public interest objectives could be impeded;
- in the interests of protecting judicial independence and the conduct of judicial proceedings;
- investigations, detection and proceeding conducted by professional organisations in relation to matters of conduct or ethics;
- other monitoring, inspection and regulatory functions;
- the protection of other data subjects or the rights and freedoms of others; and
- civil law enforcement.

6. The right to have data corrected or updated
Article 16 of the GDPR gives data subjects the right to have inaccurate data rectified. In certain circumstances, rectification extends to requiring the data controller to amend personal data that is

"The second decade of this millennium has marked a key period in the development of the concept [usually known as 'the right to be forgotten'], which is enshrined in the GDPR."

incomplete (provided that this is pertinent to the processing being undertaken by that data controller).

While the request for correction can be made orally or in writing, it is clearly prudent for the data controller to confirm in writing to the data subject the steps being taken in response to a request of this kind.

Where data was incorrectly provided by the data subject, common sense prevails and there is no breach (subject to what is said below on the duty to ensure that data is kept up to date, which would prompt the data subject to offer a correction). The data controller does not need to carry out any verification activities under data protection law. By contrast, an interesting example provided in the ICO guidance concerning rights of rectification covers circumstances in which a patient receiving medical treatment is initially misdiagnosed, but the diagnosis is subsequently made correctly. The existence of the misdiagnosis involves a statement of fact valid at the time it was made and should therefore not be corrected.

The right of rectification relates very closely to the duty to ensure that personal data held is accurate, which is a requirement of Article 5(1)(d) and covered in Chapter III of this Special Report.

The duty to hold accurate data is an ongoing one to be complied with by the data controller. For this reason, organisations with a likely longer-term relationship with a data subject must have a process in place to resubmit the information to the data subject in order to offer him/her the opportunity to update the data. This action will be particularly important when information is sourced from a third party – meaning that its accuracy cannot be entirely verified.

7. Must a request for rectification always be responded to?

Perhaps surprisingly, the answer is 'no' and a range of circumstances can arise in which a request might be regarded as manifestly unfounded. The ICO guidance cites an array of situations in which a request may be disregarded, including where:

- the individual is not in practice exercising the right – for example, an individual making a request and then offering to withdraw the request for financial compensation; or
- the request is malicious with evidence of this in the request.

8. The right to have personal data deleted

With the rise of social media, it came as no surprise that a concept usually known as 'the right to be forgotten' emerged. The second decade of this millennium has marked a key period in the development of the concept, which is enshrined in the GDPR.

"One of the most common questions raised in the early days of the GDPR was the position to be taken in relation to backup systems. The law is silent on how to comply where backup copies contain the personal data to be erased."

Article 17 provides for the principle of data erasure. The right is qualified in terms of the ability to require erasure.

The circumstances in which erasure can be requested and must be complied with are as follows:

- The personal data is no longer necessary for the purpose for which it was originally collected;
- The personal data was collected by consent and the consent is withdrawn, and there is no other lawful basis to process the personal data;
- Where legitimate interest is the basis relied upon for processing, but on balance there is no overriding legitimate interest for continuing to process;
- Under direct marketing activities, the individual objects to the processing;
- The personal data has been processed unlawfully; and
- There is a requirement to erase personal data under a legal obligation.

9. Personal data in the hands of third parties – is any action required?

Where any of the personal data has been made available to a third party, the data controller is under a duty to contact recipients of the data (this would seem to be whether they are processing the data under the data controller's instructions or have received it for any other legitimate data-sharing arrangement). The duty does not require to be fulfilled if notification would be impossible or would involve disproportionate effort.

Where the data subject requests information concerning the identity of third parties that may hold any of the personal data concerned, this request should be responded to.

10. What about data backup systems?

One of the most common questions raised in the early days of the GDPR was the position to be taken in relation to backup systems. The law is silent on how to comply where backup copies contain the personal data to be erased. The ICO in its guidance takes a relatively strong line on the matter. While recognising that in most cases there is little risk of a data breach when personal data sits in a backup environment, the data controller must nonetheless have a system in place that ensures that the data concerned is erased in due course. This could be through the overwriting of a backup with a fresh backup copy in accordance with the security procedures of the data controller.

11. The data subject requests restriction on the processing of personal data

This lesser-known right of a data subject can be found in Article 18 of the GDPR. The right of restriction enables a data subject to require that personal data held should either not be processed or processed only within limitations set by the data subject. The data subject is entitled to make the restriction request on the following grounds:

- Accuracy has been queried and the data controller is investigating;
- Data has been unlawfully processed and the data subject prefers restriction to erasure;
- The data controller has no continuing need for the data, but the data subject wishes the data to be retained in order to establish, exercise or defend a legal claim; or
- The data controller wishes to retain and process the data on legitimate interest grounds, but the data subject has objected – the restriction must be applied pending resolution of the issue.

12. Data portability

In recent years there has been significant campaigning around the benefits for an individual of being able to require the transfer of personal data held by or on behalf of a data controller to the data subject or to another data controller – the latter being relevant if, for example, a service such as internet banking is involved.

Article 20 of the GDPR entitles a data subject to require the provision of personal data in a format that meets the requirement of being in a structure commonly used and in a machine-readable format. The right is limited to personal data provided by the data subject and which is processed by automated means, and the basis of the processing relied upon has been either consent or the performance of a contract with the data subject.

The right may not be exercised in certain circumstances, notably where the personal data has been developed by or for the data controller in connection with its legitimate interests or for purposes that relate to complying with a legal obligation or are associated with discharging a public function.

13. Automated decision making

The increasing use of automated decision-making systems – typically powered by artificial intelligence (AI) – leads to this final right provided to data subjects. Article 22 of the GDPR grants data subjects rights associated with automatic decision making that are likely to have a significant impact on the data subject.

The role of AI and the challenges it creates for data protection are explained in Chapter XIII.

Reference has to be made to Recital 72 of the EU GDPR, which provides some background to this right as it suggests its relevance in circumstances such as credit approvals, e-recruiting and work-related automatic profiling.

There is a right (with exceptions) not to be subjected to decision making of this kind. The exceptions are set out in Article 22(2) and are as follows:

- The processing is necessary for entering into or performing a contract between the data subject and the data controller;
- There is legislative authority for the processing, provided the legislative authority is set against appropriate protective measures for the data subject; and
- The data subject has given explicit consent.

An important proviso to these grounds is that in all cases the data controller must be able to show that suitable measures are in place to safeguard the data subject's rights and freedoms and legitimate interests, and the data subject has the right to obtain human intervention, allowing for the expression of the data subject's point of view concerning the decision taken and to contest the decision.

Should an organisation look to apply automated decision making, it will be expected to have in place protections for the benefit of the data subject that should include:

- being able to demonstrate that the decision making took place in a fair and transparent manner;
- using reliable and appropriate mathematical or statistical processes;
- implementing appropriate technical and organisation measures to limit inaccuracy and to provide for error correction; and
- securing the personal data in a manner proportionate to risks that could arise and avoiding discriminatory outcomes.

XII. The role of the Information Commissioner's Office and data protection enforcement

1. Introduction

The stated aim of the Information Commissioner's Office (ICO) is "to uphold information rights for the UK public in the digital age".[43]

The commissioner holds office for a term of up to seven years. No person appointed can be reappointed to the position for a second term.[44]

The legal status of an information commissioner is that of a corporation sole – giving the organisation legal identity in the name of the appointed commissioner. The duties of the commissioner are delegated to the ICO Board.

As will be explained in this chapter, the ICO's role is broader than being the regulator for data protection – it encompasses numerous functions. In its regulatory role, the ICO has not just a civil-based jurisdiction but also powers of criminal prosecution. The manner in which the ICO operates its civil and criminal sanctions powers are also explored later in this chapter.

Public oversight of the ICO is through the Department for Digital, Culture, Media and Sport, with the working relationship between the two established through a management agreement assuring funding for the ICO but at the same time independence in the conduct of its functions.

2. Constitution and functions of the ICO

Schedules 12 and 13 of the Data Protection Act 2018 are relevant to understanding the full extent of the role played by the ICO.

Schedule 12 establishes the legal basis for continuity of the ICO subsequent to the repeal of the Data Protection Act 1998. The commissioner is required to appoint deputy commissioners; where more than one deputy commissioner is appointed, the specific functions delegated to each need to be formalised within the appointment.

Funding, as already noted, is provisioned through the Department for Digital, Culture, Media and Sport. Importantly, receipts arising from registration fees, charges, penalties and other sums received are all to be accounted for to the department's secretary of state.

The functions of the commissioner are specified in Schedule 13 of the Data Protection Act 2018. In brief, these are:

- to monitor and enforce provisions of the Data Protection Act 2018 (and, effectively, the GDPR) relating to data subject rights and compliance by data controllers and data processors with their legal obligations;
- an educational role that recognises the continuing need to develop understanding of the impact of, in particular, technology on personal data – this duty is set out in Schedule 13(1)(2);
- to "promote public awareness and understanding of the risks, rules, safeguards and rights in relation to processing of personal data";
- to advise Parliament, the government and other institutions and bodies of legislative and administrative measures relating to the protection of individuals' rights and freedoms with regard to processing of personal data;
- in relation to data controllers and data processors, to promote the awareness of obligations that exist under data protection legislation;
- to provide a helpdesk-type support for the general public over matters concerning data protection;
- to cooperate with international organisations;
- to conduct investigations into data protection compliance matters; and
- to monitor developments in technology that have an impact on the protection of personal data.

"There is now no duty to maintain a register of data controllers as was previously required under Section 19 of the Data Protection Act 1998. The absence of a register is a consequence of this requirement not being included in the EU GDPR."

Until 31 January 2020 the ICO had a responsibility to participate in the European Data Protection Board – the EU body that provides a valuable coordination and guidance-forming function for EU member states. With the UK membership of the EU ending on 31 January 2020, rights to participate ceased.

There is now no duty to maintain a register of data controllers as was previously required under Section 19 of the Data Protection Act 1998. The absence of a register is a consequence of this requirement not being included in the EU GDPR.

The UK, however, determined that there should continue to be visibility of organisations that process personal data. The Data Protection (Charges and Information) Regulations 2018 (amended with effect from 1 April 2019) came into force on 25 May 2018, requiring organisations (and individuals) concerned with the processing of personal data to pay an annual fee prescribed by the regulations. As of September 2020, the fee applied is established on a banded basis ranging from £40 to £2,900 – the appropriate band determined by reference to a range of criteria including employee numbers and turnover. Public authorities, charities and small occupational pension schemes are banded by reference to more specific criteria relevant to the nature of the organisation.

Failure on the part of a data controller or data processor to register exposes the party concerned to a fine not exceeding (as of September 2020) £4,350.

3. Development of guidance and codes of practice

The ICO will in the course of its function to develop the general public understanding of data protection publish guidance and other forms of information to meet the needs of its audience.

Under the Data Protection Act 2018, the ICO is also tasked with a duty to publish codes of practice that are to have statutory force. The specific codes to be published can be found in Table 6.

To understand the role that codes of practice play, reference needs to be made to Section 127 of the Data Protection Act 2018. Under that provision:

- failure to comply does not *per se* lead to any form of civil or criminal liability;
- the code is however admissible evidence in any legal proceedings; and
- it is a matter for the court to decide whether any provision in

Table 6. Codes of practice

Code name	Statutory provision for the code	Current status of the code
Data Sharing Code	Section 121(1)	The code is in final form having been submitted to the Secretary of State for Digital, Culture, Media and Sport to lay before Parliament. It can be expected to come into effect later in 2021.
Direct Marketing Code	Section 122	The code is in draft form for consultation purposes.
Age Appropriate Design Code	Section 123	This code came into force on 2 September 2020.
Data Protection and Journalism Code	Section 124	Consultation pre-development of a draft of the code has been completed.

> the code put forward as relevant to the proceedings is, indeed, relevant to the matter before the court.

The codes are also relevant to the performance of the ICO's functions; Section 127(4) of the Data Protection Act provides that in carrying out its functions the ICO must take into account a provision of a code where, again, that provision is relevant to the function being carried out.

4. The investigatory function of the ICO

The ICO operates its investigatory function at both a formal and an informal level. An outline of the powers of the ICO is set out next. More detail on the matters covered may be found in the ICO Regulatory Action Policy[45] (discussed in more detail later in this chapter).

Informally, the ICO may – in accordance with Section 129 of the Data Protection Act 2018 – decide, with the consent of the relevant party, to carry out an assessment of whether the data controller or data processor is following good practice in the processing of personal data. This is referred to as a consensual audit. A form of engagement letter is put in place setting out the scope of the audit and the expectations that the ICO has for cooperation in the exercise.

The ICO is required to inform the data controller or data processor of the results of the assessment. Where it is in the public interest, the ICO will also publish a high-level overview of the findings of the audit.

Formal investigatory and associated enforcement powers are provided for in Part 6 of the Data Protection Act 2018.

To give the ICO an effective basis to take forward any concerns over data protection compliance, a broad power is provided so that the ICO may seek and obtain information from data controllers and data processors. Legal privilege is, however, respected.

The ICO may request of a data controller or data processor information that the ICO "reasonably requires"[46] in order to carry out any investigation of either a possible failure in data protection compliance or a suspected offence under the Data Protection Act 2018.

To be valid, the information notice must be issued in connection with one of the following potential failings on the part of the recipient of the notice:

- a breach of duties as a data controller or data processor in relation to processing duties;

"When the EU GDPR was introduced, much emphasis was placed by commentators and others on the high level of penalties that regulators were now empowered to levy."

- a breach of duty owed to data subjects individually;
- certain specific provisions of the GDPR that impose duties – namely, Articles 25 to 39, which are the detailed provisions setting out the duties of data controllers and data processors, and Chapter 4 of the Data Protection Act 2018, which covers further requirements of data controllers and data processors;
- failure to notify a data protection breach to the ICO or a data subject; and
- matters associated with transfers of personal data to third countries.

Non-cooperation can lead to the ICO taking the matter to court, with the consequence that compliance with the information notice may be supported by an enforcement notice. Penalty provisions apply where information provided proves to be false.

Where the ICO wishes to impose a deeper investigatory regime on a data controller or data processor, Section 146 of the Data Protection Act 2018 creates an 'assessment' regime.

The ICO will serve an assessment notice on the target organisation. This may require the data controller or data processor to respond in a number of ways, which can include all or any of the following:

- provide access to premises as specified by the ICO;
- provide access to types of documents specified by the ICO;
- provide access to information specified by the ICO in machine-readable format;
- provide copies of documents and information as required by the ICO;
- provide the ICO with access to equipment or other material on the premises of a specified description with related powers of examination available to the ICO and requirements to provide explanations;
- permit the commissioner to observe processing operations on the premises; and/or
- make available people of a specified description who process personal data on behalf of the controller (where a data controller is the subject of the assessment) who are willing to be interviewed.

An assessment exercise does, of course, require cooperation on the part of the controller or processor. To secure that cooperation, recourse can be had to the High Court to obtain a warrant to enter and search premises of the party that is the subject of an assessment notice.

5. Regulatory Action Policy

The ICO fulfils its regulatory functions guided by its Regulatory Action Policy.[47] The stated purpose of the policy (found in its introductory overview) is "to provide direction and focus for those we regulate, the public and our staff about our chosen approach to regulatory action".

Awareness of this document is valuable. When the EU GDPR was introduced, much emphasis was placed by commentators and others on the high level of penalties that regulators were now empowered to levy. The emphasis on these maximum penalties means little in practice because relatively few organisations will be exposed to them, compared to the vast number of others which are also subject to regulation.

The Regulatory Action Policy provides an overview of the approach to be taken to regulation (with steps that can be taken falling short of imposing a financial penalty or seeking a criminal prosecution).

The criteria that will be adopted can be seen in Table 7.

Table 7. Criteria adopted by the ICO in relation to data breaches

Consideration	Impact
Nature and seriousness of the breach	The nature and seriousness of the breach or potential breach (including, for example, whether any critical national infrastructure or service is involved)
The personal data affected with consideration given to its character	Where relevant, the categories of personal data affected (including whether any special category personal data is involved) and the level of any privacy intrusion
The quantum of data subjects affected and impact on those individuals	The number of individuals affected, the extent of any exposure to physical, financial or psychological harm and, where it is an issue, the degree of intrusion into their privacy
Novelty of the issues, the existence of repetition and any technological issues leading to the personal data breach	Whether the issue raises new or repeated issues, or concerns that technological security measures are not protecting the personal data
Gravity and duration of the breach	The gravity and duration of a breach or potential breach
Likelihood of repetition of the issue giving concern	Whether the organisation or individual involved is representative of a sector or group, raising the possibility of similar issues arising again across that group or sector if not addressed
Cost of mitigation	The cost of measures to mitigate any risk, issue or harm
Public interest in any action taken	The public interest in regulatory action being taken (eg, to provide an effective deterrent against future breaches or clarify or test an issue in dispute)
Consideration of regulatory or law enforcement action taken by others	Whether another regulator, law enforcement body or competent authority is already taking (or has already taken) action in respect of the same matter
European Data Protection Board opinions relevant to the matter	For circumstances arising in the period during which the EU GDPR continued to apply in the UK, 'expressed opinions' of the European Data Protection Board are also considered to be relevant

The ICO also reserves the right to take into account any aggravating or mitigating factors where relevant.

6. What might constitute an 'aggravating factor'?
Examples offered in the Regulatory Action Policy include the existence of an intentional, wilful or negligent approach to compliance, the operation of an unlawful business or operating model, and whether prior advice, warnings or guidance – including, where relevant, from the organisation's DPO – has been followed. Where children's data is involved, an important recognised aggravating factor is "the vulnerability ... of individuals affected".

7. Factors taken as mitigation
The Regulatory Action Policy also offers mitigating factors; the examples given include whether any code of conduct has been followed, how promptly the organisation reacted to the circumstances, and the state and nature of protective or preventative measures and technology adopted.

8. Factors taken into account to calculate a penalty
In any situation where a penalty is to be levied, the Regulatory Action Policy identifies a step-by-step approach under which the circumstances receive a careful assessment. The following five steps are to be considered, so far as relevant:

- an 'initial element' removing any financial gain from the breach;
- adding in an element to censure the breach based on its scale and severity, taking into account the considerations identified at Sections 155(2)-(4) of the Data Protection Act 2018;
- adding in an element to reflect any aggravating factors;
- adding in an amount for deterrent effect to others; and
- reducing the amount (save that in the initial element) to reflect any mitigating factors, including ability to pay (financial hardship).

Importantly, in cases involving failure to meet data security obligations the ICO considers any reporting failure separately from the breach itself. This means that even a minor breach could be subject to a more severe sanction than might be expected if the breach is not notified in accordance with the requirements for notification under Article 34 of the GDPR.

In its application of the above process, the ICO will consider:

- whether there has been an impact on vulnerable individuals;
- whether a deliberate action has been taken to achieve any financial gain;

- whether any warning signals – contained in advice, guidance, recommendations or warning (including those from a DPO) – have been disregarded;
- whether there is a high degree of intrusion into the privacy of data subjects;
- whether there has been a failure to cooperate with the ICO investigatory powers or any enforcement action; and
- whether the target of the investigation shows a pattern of poor regulatory history.

9. Criminal prosecution policy

The ICO is vested with powers to instigate criminal prosecutions in a number of circumstances. Most relevant is the power to prosecute individuals who are responsible for data protection breaches.

The powers available to the ICO extend throughout the UK as data protection is not a devolved matter; the courts in each UK jurisdiction may thus be used for prosecution purposes.

10. Power to impose penalties and the courts' powers to fine – what might a breach cost?

Both civil and criminal penalties can arise from failures to comply with data protection legislation. We will take each in turn.

10.1 Civil penalties

These are governed by the GDPR as moderated by the ICO Regulatory Action Policy and considerations that are taken into account. Despite the move from the EU GDPR to the UK GDPR, the maximum penalty continues to be stated in Euros and remains, for the present, at €20 million or 4% of turnover, whichever is greater.[48]

10.2 Criminal penalties

A number of criminal offences are associated with data protection legislation. The most relevant are outlined below.

(a) Section 179 of the Data Protection Act 2018

This section provides that it is an offence (previously set out in Section 55 of the Data Protection Act 1998 but with a subtle increase in scope) for a person knowingly or recklessly:

- to obtain or disclose personal data without the consent of the controller;
- to procure the disclosure of personal data to another person without the consent of the controller; or
- after obtaining personal data, to retain it without the consent of the person who was the controller in relation to the personal data when it was obtained (this is new in the 2018 act).

The addition of the third limb clearly increases the ante in the context of provisions within the GDPR regime associated with data minimisation, the duty to have a data deletion policy and to apply that policy in practice.

Criminal prosecution is however more likely in circumstances where individuals extract data for their own personal gain; in the past, cases that have come to court have included employees in sales or marketing positions taking customer data to a new employer to use to the advantage of that employee and the future employer.

(b) Section 184

This provision concerns data subject access requests. The section (previously found at Section 56 of the Data Protection Act 1998) prohibits organisations from attempting to utilise the access request regime to support background checks on an individual. The section also prohibits requesting access to or the provision of records protected under data protection legislation.

(c) Section 171

This section provides a new offence under the Data Protection Act 2018 – promoted following a recommendation by Dame Fiona Caldicott, National Guardian for Health and Care – by criminalising the re-identification of personal data that has been de-identified through, for example, redactions.

(d) Section 173

The final offence of note is one that can arise when an organisation becomes subject to a duty to disclose information to the ICO. It is an offence under Section 173 to alter, deface, block erase or conceal information with the intention of preventing its disclosure.

Case study

The *Leo Kirk* prosecution

The ICO reserves a section of its website to provide information on actions taken in circumstances in which data subjects rights have been breached. A growing number of prosecutions of individuals who have had access to personal data in connection with their employment is noted. Once case concerned Leo Kirk, a former social worker who was prosecuted for passing the personal information of service users to a third-party provider for local authority young person placements.

The ICO noted that:

> *Leo Kirk unlawfully disclosed referrals for residential or foster placements of vulnerable young people aged 16-18 years old.*

The referrals contained sensitive personal data including potential identifier information and vulnerability risks of the service user.

A fine of £483 was imposed. Kirk was also ordered to pay costs of £364.08 and a victim surcharge of £48.[49]

11. Promoting the development and implementation of accreditation schemes and codes of conduct

A final role to be played by the information commissioner is:

- to promote and oversee schemes that provide for the accreditation or certification of parties which are data processors or data controllers; and
- to provide codes of conduct that particular organisations agree to adhere to.

Under accreditation schemes, individuals or organisations with responsibilities under data protection legislation are certified as meeting particular standards. Such certification offers the advantage of more efficient due diligence, enabling, for example, a data controller to entrust data processing to a particular party that is certified without further investigation.

Codes of conduct are likely to be of particular interest to industry bodies (eg, trade associations). Detailed guidance as to how to participate in the schemes (which many will consider demanding in their requirements) is published on the ICO website.[50]

XIII. Artificial intelligence and data protection

1. Introduction

The application of artificial intelligence (AI) to support and, in an increasing number of situations, to actually make decisions based on or taking account of an individual's personal data has become a significant issue given the tension that inevitably arises when trying to protect an individual's data while also encouraging innovation across a vast array of disciplines and business activities.

There is an increasing body of evidence to support the contention that AI applications are good. Developments in health have been particularly notable. Large-scale analysis of anonymised data is now well understood to lead to important clinical and other public health outcomes of huge value to society. Announcements are frequently made about medical advances, such as that concerning the diagnosis of breast cancer where an AI-based interrogation of a scan is said to have a greater probability of identifying cancer than the equivalent human scrutiny.

AI necessarily involves the collection, storage and use of vast amounts of data – the term 'Big Data' is frequently used to describe the environment we now live in – within which we should start to have expectations that our personal data is highly valuable in the greater sense than to us as individuals and that we should view the processing of that data positively, as intended for the greater good.

The concept of the harvesting of personal data is, of course, contrary to key principles of data protection legislation, such as acting with the consent – or at least knowledge – of the data subject and the principle of data minimisation.

AI models, as we shall see, have at their heart the availability of large amounts of data. And the source of that data (any individual who may be a witting or unwitting contributor) becomes, of course, irrelevant. Personal data, as it is taken into an AI application, can and should become anonymised for the purposes of machine learning-based processing.

But that process of data collection and conversion into an anonymised state, together with questions about the use of AI, the integrity of its use and the validity of its outcomes, is an area that remains controversial – sufficiently so for the ICO to have allocated significant resources to the issue and dedicated a team to support both the regulation and dissemination of sound guidance and good practice in this field.

This chapter explores the data protection issues associated with the use of AI and its role in profiling. The subject of profiling has been covered more generally elsewhere. But first, the answer to the question of what is meant by AI.

"AI models, as we shall see, have at their heart the availability of large amounts of data. And the source of that data (any individual who may be a witting or unwitting contributor) becomes, of course, irrelevant."

Case study

The role played by data analytics companies

An even broader concept than AI is that known as 'Big Data'. Technological advances have created the possibility of retaining vast amounts of data at very low cost. Much of that data will have a potential value in the development of AI-based models, but it also has value in the ability to produce statistics in a highly sophisticated way.

Departing from the subject of AI for the moment, this aspect is also of interest to the ICO, which has produced discussion papers on the subject of Big Data, most recently in 2016.[51]

Examples quoted by the ICO in its discussion paper include companies that have the capability to trawl publicly available online sources such as Twitter, Linkedin and Facebook, extracting data of value for marketing purposes.

Geotagging, which has become particularly prevalent, forms a further frontier in the advance of data collection opportunities – for example, photos posted to Instagram with their link to the contributor are known to have been processed to deliver sound estimates of visitor numbers at tourist sites and (significantly) where the visitors have come from. Mobile phone presence data can be used to analyse the footfall in retail centres and most recently was used by the UK government in briefings relating to lockdown, to demonstrate significant reductions in travel patterns.

2. What is AI?

At the heart of any use of AI is the process known as machine learning. Large amounts of data will be fed into a computer system that has powerful processing capabilities. The computer processing enables the computer to assimilate the data and, in doing so, to learn how to carry out accurately a task that it has been directed to complete. This could be the identification of an individual using perhaps just a single image capture of that individual or the recognition of the speech of an individual (taking into account language spoken but also accent), converting that speech into written words.

In more detail, machine learning involves a process of training using neural network technology. A neural network exists in the form of a series of interconnected layers of algorithms, each layer being identified as a neuron. The neurons deliver data into each other in a process of training to carry out the required tasks – adjusting the weighting attributed to input data automatically as it passes between the neuron layers. The processing instructions enable the weightings attached to inputs undergoing processing to be varied on a trial-and-

"Not all data that is fed into AI models will be personal data, but for many significant uses there will be personal data – albeit usually stripped of the elements that can present a link to the data subject. This is the essential step of anonymisation."

error basis until the output from the neural network achieves the expected output – or is as close to that as is possible. The optimum process (with the data value weightings established) is then set. At that point, the network will have 'learned' how to carry out a particular task.

When implemented, the model that has been developed reacts to relevant information that is provided to it with no human intervention – delivering an outcome that, in many uses of AI, may be a decision that can be provided to the data subject with no human intervention.

In practice, three potential outcomes arise from the use of AI:

- a prediction – the characteristics of an individual (eg, the likelihood of defaulting on a financial commitment such as a bank loan);
- a recommendation – what the individual should do next when engaging with the model (eg, a learning experience); or
- a classification – determining how a particular piece of information should be categorised.

3. What are the issues with AI?

Not all data that is fed into AI models will be personal data, but for many significant uses there will be personal data – albeit usually stripped of the elements that can present a link to the data subject. This is the essential step of anonymisation.

The data then loses its personal data status. There is, however, an intermediate step that can be taken in the processing of data known as 'pseudonymisation' – a process of separating elements of the data that specifically identifies an individual from other data necessarily being collected. There will be many circumstances in which it is necessary to maintain a link – such as where the data is being processed on a basis that requires reporting of outcomes specific to the individual.

Case study

AI and the role of human intervention

A healthtech business has developed a basis for accurately interpreting digitised scans to diagnose a health condition. To use the process, the scan and certain other clinically significant information are fed into the system and processed to produce an outcome. The outcome is then linked back to the identity of the patient.

The data fed into the model may well remain within the model (together with clinician input assessing how accurate the outcome was found to be) in order to provide ever more accurate outcomes in the future. In the meantime, a link to the personal identifying data necessarily has to remain in place.

For so long as that position remains, all of the data is compositely still regarded as personal data and requires protection as such.

For the data subject who is then profiled using the collected data, there is the issue of accountability. Decisions taken by a business manager are clearly attributable to an individual. Where AI is applied in the decision making and processes completed without human intervention, the story is different and accountability a more complex matter.

4. Use of personal data under AI conditions is likely to constitute 'profiling'

Under the GDPR 'profiling' is described as involving:

> *any form of automated processing of Personal Data consisting of using those data to evaluate certain personal aspects relating to a natural person, in particular to analyse or predict aspects concerning that natural person's performance at work, economic situation, health, personal preferences, interests, reliability, behaviour, location or movements.*[52]

"Data protection laws are not about preventing the use of personal data in innovative ways: the UK legislation in that regard is instead about being transparent about the personal data collected and the purposes for which it is intended to be processed, and enabling data subjects to maintain overall control."

Article 22 of the GDPR prescribes that individuals should not be subjected to purely automated decision making if it "significantly affects" the individual. The GDPR provides three important qualifications:

- the data subject has consented to the profiling;
- the profiling is authorised by law; or
- the profiling is associated with performance of a contract with the data subject.

Profiling in the case of children has further considerations that we looked at in Chapter VIII.

5. Decisions taken using AI must be explainable
Perhaps the greatest challenge is that of translating sophisticated, mathematically denominated, operational computer systems into simplified explanations that data subjects will readily understand and in relation to which they will be able to make informed decisions. The GDPR requirement to enable a data subject to require human intervention in the decision making[53] implies that the process should be one that is understood, with human intervention to be seen as a safeguard assuring a comprehensible outcome. To limit demands for human intervention, service providers that take advantage of AI-based decision making clearly have an incentive to be able to articulate how decisions are made under AI.

6. Impact on the principle of data minimisation
Given the logistics associated with the storing of data and the potential high level of processing power available to a data controller, the opportunities to use data to maximum effect – and to find ever new ways of using data – make the issue of data minimisation of great importance.

As is often said, data protection laws are not about preventing the use of personal data in innovative ways: the UK legislation in that regard is instead about being transparent about the personal data collected and the purposes for which it is intended to be processed, and enabling data subjects to maintain overall control.

Where a new opportunity arises to apply personal data held, great care needs to be taken in deciding to proceed. Is this a purpose for which the data could be argued to have been collected in the first place? Would the data subject have contemplated that new purpose when giving consent (if that is how the personal data was collected)? Should a fresh consent be taken to cover this issue?

These questions will come to the fore in the thinking of the data controller if it follows the expectations of the ICO and conducts a data protection impact assessment to establish and consider the risks associated with a particular proposed new project.

Data protection impact assessments were explained in Chapter X. It is the view of the ICO that all uses of AI should usually be preceded by a data protection impact assessment.[54] Furthermore, where an organisation introduces into a project an AI model that has been developed by a third party, that impact assessment cannot start from the basis that the model adopted is sound – due diligence should be undertaken to be sure that is the case.

7. Fairness in processing

While the role of the ICO is to regulate data protection matters, this is not to the exclusion of other citizens' rights and, in particular, those arising under equalities legislation. A key risk that has been recognised in the development of AI models is bias, where the data that has been used to train the model does not have sufficient diversity in the make-up of data subjects to produce a truly balanced outcome – in short, the data set cannot be regarded as representative of the population as a whole. A detailed consideration to this issue is provided by the ICO in its Explaining Decisions Made with AI.[55]

8. The importance of explaining decisions when using AI

Not all uses of AI involve the direct making of decisions that have an impact on the data subject. The use of AI in marketing is an example where purchasing habits are surveyed and processed, and judgements made that lead to targeted advertising.

But where the profiling that is conducted does lead to decisions being made, the role of AI in that comes centre stage and requires that the user of the AI model provide an informed and meaningful explanation of how the decision was reached.

9. Duration within which data is held

As already discussed in Chapter XI, the ability to store large quantities of data at limited cost has to be reconciled with the expectation that personal data is retained only for the minimum period necessary; its conversion into an anonymised form with the consent of the data subject does, of course, address that point.

10. Ability to respond to data subject rights

In planning to use personal data within an AI model, a key consideration will be the ability, when required, to respond accurately to the data subject rights (explained in Chapter XI). The use of a well-developed data protection impact assessment will include considerations of this kind and how the data subject rights are protected.

11. How the ICO approaches AI

As mentioned at the beginning of this chapter, the ICO pays particular attention to the use of AI and its interface with data protection. A series of blogs have appeared on the ICO website with the intention of stimulating discussion around the tensions between taking advantage of Big Data-based opportunities and data protection.

From a regulatory standpoint, the ICO is well prepared to address circumstances in which it has concerns about the use of AI and where actual complaints are received. A toolkit has been published that covers:

- the ICO's approach to the auditing of circumstances in which AI is applied to personal data;[56] and
- explainability in the use of AI and personal data.[57]

XIV. Data protection post-Brexit – the hot topics

1. Introduction

The framework of data protection legislation that takes the UK into the post-Brexit age will form the background for many issues that frequently require attention in our court system. The year 2020 for instance saw a significant case on employer responsibility for wrongful actions of staff who compromise personal data reaching the Supreme Court (see section 2 below).

The issue of what freedoms there should be to transfer data outside of the UK's data protection system is another area of continuing contention.

As noted earlier in this Special Report, the increasing role of AI in the processing of personal data has opened up another battlefront between data privacy campaigners and promoters of innovative solutions for many of the challenges that society confronts, including health, good educational outcomes and even policing.

A particularly controversial application of AI-based systems that affects the life of virtually every computer and smartphone user is behavioural-based advertising, where the user's interests expressed through online activity are captured, processed and turned into

"The [Supreme Court] judgment [in Morrisons*] sends a message to all employers that the issue of vicarious liability remains a potential route to compensation for a data subject."*

targeted advertising promoting products and services highly likely to be of interest. The topic has become even more controversial with service providers such as Google even interrogating email content (with its Gmail product) as part of their tracking of user behaviours.

In this final chapter we look at these areas and how the ICO endeavours to appropriately balance the encouragement of innovation with the protection of the rights of the individual data subjects. This chapter also looks at a case in which the courts had to navigate tricky waters to the background of a significant data breach, leading to a class action by a large group of affected individuals and the long-standing rule that employers can be vicariously liable for the wrongful actions of employees.

2. The *WM Morrison Supermarkets plc* case[58]

When a massive data protection breach involves a major employer as its direct victim and more than 5,500 personnel as collateral damage, it is no surprise that this leads to a major civil case taken up to the highest decision-making court in the UK – the Supreme Court.

The case concerned a disgruntled employee of WM Morrison Supermarkets plc (trading as Morrisons) with a very high-level access to the data of the business due to his involvement in the internal audit function. Having resigned from the business in unhappy circumstances, the employee – Andrew Skelton – chose a dramatic way of demonstrating disenchantment with his former employer. On leaving he took with him the personal data of the company's personnel, later making this accessible through a public file-sharing website.

A class action raised against Morrisons was initially successful, with the High Court finding in favour of the plaintiffs – the basis for this being the long-established rule that an employer should be found responsible for actions engaged in by an employee where third parties suffer loss.

The Supreme Court reversed this decision, but in doing so scrutinised the circumstances and careful consideration of how far employee Skelton had departed from the usual course of his duties owed to his employer.

While the Supreme Court decision went in favour of Morrisons, the judgment given by Lord Toulson sends a message to all employers that the issue of vicarious liability remains a potential route to compensation for a data subject with particular regard being had to the function that the employee performed within the organisation and the degree of connection between the wrongdoing that occurred and the functions performed by the employee. In short, the question is: was the wrongdoing sufficiently closely connected to the role played by the employee for the employer to be found liable?

It seems likely that cases of this kind will arise again. Employees losing data sticks, leaving computer monitors on close to windows and working on documents electronically on trains are just three examples of risks that employers will routinely encounter.

As we saw in Chapter X, information governance is an area that demands close attention on the part of organisations to ensure that effective procedures are in place to minimise, or even eliminate, risks of this kind.

3. The impact of Brexit, including the relevance of data protection to the effective conclusion of trade deals

One of issues that had been the focus of attention during the period in which arrangements were being made with the EU for the UK's departure from EU membership was whether the EU will judge the UK's data protection legislation as affording adequate protection for EU citizens. The issue is of significance because having an adequacy decision leads to a streamlining of transfers of data from the EU to the UK as a 'third country'. Without such a decision, transfers of personal data from the EU to UK organisations will require additional legal safeguards – usually referred to as 'standard contractual clauses' – and the taking of increased due diligence steps relating to the security of the data and limitations on other parties (eg, surveillance authorities) to access the data.

Standard contractual clauses are a set of requirements that may be bolted into commercial or other contractual agreements that would lead to a UK data processor committing to protect personal data in terms that meet the expectations for protection set within the EU under the EU GDPR.

The EU committed to support the securing of an adequacy decision within the Brexit political declaration, but the decision making on previous adequacy decisions (11 have been made in relation to other non-EU or EEA countries) can be lengthy – 18 months being the record to date and with the timeline for the EU and UK being significantly shorter.

By contrast, the UK has made it clear that it regards the EU data protection regime as adequate, with data controllers free, accordingly, to transfer data to EU entities without additional formal data protection compliance clauses of the kind the EU expects of the UK.

Protection of personal data is now an important consideration in all free trade arrangements given the increasing role played by digital services in international trade. The UK having adopted its own version of the EU GDPR will make this aspect one of the most straightforward issues to consider when negotiating trade deals with other countries across the world.

4. Advertising and personal data

This is one of two particularly controversial areas concerning the use of personal data – the second, facial recognition technology, being addressed in section 5 below.

The EU is developing legislation to regulate behavioural advertising – the EU Parliament in particular having been subjected to intensive and sustained lobbying on the issue. The argument is that there is a growing propensity for individuals to be targeted under mass surveillance strategies that connect potential advertisers to sales opportunities on a customised basis involving the use of personal data.

The processes that lead to the placing on webpages of what some describe as 'personalised advertising' has become a significant economic activity with powerful technology harnessed, enabling businesses to apply their marketing budgets to real-time bidding processes, with advertisers given access to website visitors almost in

"Protection of personal data is now an important consideration in all free trade arrangements given the increasing role played by digital services in international trade."

real time against the subject of the browsing that the user has engaged in.

Regulators across the EU are carefully scrutinising the practices adopted in the context of GDPR compliance. A preliminary finding of the Belgium regulator is understood to have found that a tool used by digital marketing and advertising association IAB Europe to secure user consent fails to meet the GDPR requirements, placing that business in a position in which all the processing it embarks on is unlawful.[59]

In the UK, the ICO published an updated report on this activity (described as 'adtech') in June 2019.[60] The ICO expresses considerable caution over the practices adopted and is now engaged in further research with a view to reaching conclusions that it considers appropriate. A particular concern surrounds the access gained to data subject special category data – an implication being that data controllers will have difficulties demonstrating that the greater requirements for consent to the use of such data have been met.

The data profiles that are created through the processing of personal data are referred to in the report as sometimes "disproportionate, intrusive and unfair, particularly when people are often unaware that it is happening".[61]

Behavioural advertising is recognised as a marketing tool of advantage to businesses both large and small. It can be argued that it also benefits data subjects who are thus spared exposure to information of little or no relevance.

The issues surrounding behavioural advertising will be a significant area of controversy for some time to come.

5. Facial recognition technology

Facial recognition technology is a further area in which the application of AI is proving controversial. This is particularly so with regard to its use by police forces, with a Home Office programme encouraging the placement of cameras in areas with significant footfall, such as busy high streets and around sports stadia – the intention being to identify individuals who are of interest to the police authorities.

The technology involves capturing facial detail of data subjects which is then processed to establish whether there is a reliable match against a database of targets. A case reached the Court of Appeal in early 2020, with judgment delivered in August 2020[62] declaring the particular application of technology involved unlawful. The basis of the decision provides a useful appreciation of one of the key risks that are understood to exist in connection with the use of AI – this being in the context of equalities duties.

The Court of Appeal determined that the preparatory steps taken in the development of the system were insufficient and led to a bias against women and people of colour. The police force had also failed to conduct an adequate data protection impact assessment.

To help develop an understanding of the risks of bias and discrimination that may be inherent in AI systems, the ICO has published a blog titled "Human bias and discrimination in AI systems".[63] This provides a useful explanation of what is, in the eyes of the ICO, a key compliance issue as highlighted in Chapter XIII of this Special Report.

Notes

1 Provided for by Article 44 of the EU GDPR.
2 Part 7 of Article FINPROV.10A of the EU-UK Trade and Cooperation Agreement.
3 "A Brief History of Data Protection: where did it all start", International Network of Privacy Law Professionals, 1 June 2018.
4 Convention 108 of the Council of Europe.
5 The Data Protection, Privacy and Electronic Communications (Amendments etc) (EU Exit) Regulations 2019 as amended by the Data Protection, Privacy and Electronic Communications (Amendments etc) (EU Exit) (No 2) Regulations 2019.
6 EU Directive 2016/680 of the European Parliament and of the Council of 27 April 2016 on the protection of natural persons with regard to the processing of personal data by competent authorities for the purposes of the prevention, investigation, detection or prosecution of criminal offences or the execution of criminal penalties, and on the free movement of such data.
7 European Commission: https://ec.europa.eu/info/law/law-topic/data-protection/communication-two-years-application-general-data-protection-regulation_en.
8 The ICO has provided detailed guidance on the various approaches that may be required to international data transfers at https://ico.org.uk/for-organisations/data-protection-at-the-end-of-the-transition-period/data-protection-after-the-end-of-the-transition-period-for-small-organisations/.
9 Article 26 of the GDPR.
10 *Google Inc v Vidal Hall* [2014] EWHC Civ 92.
11 Accountability and governance: ICO, https://ico.org.uk/for-organisations/guide-to-data-protection/guide-to-the-general-data-protection-regulation-gdpr/accountability-and-governance/.
12 To be absolutely clear, there should also be privacy information available to candidates seeking employment with the data controller.
13 2009 CMLR 49.
14 European Data Protection Board website: https://edpb.europa.eu/news/national-news/2019/danish-data-protection-agency-proposes-dkk-12-million-fine-danish-taxi_en.
15 Article 28(3) of the GDPR.
16 Explained in Chapter XI.
17 *Innovations (Mail Order) Limited v Data Protection Registrar* (DA92 31/491).
18 For information on what may constitute legitimate interests, see Chapter IV (section 2.6) and the ICO website: https://ico.org.uk/for-organisations/guide-to-data-protection/guide-to-the-general-data-protection-regulation-gdpr/legitimate-interests/.
19 *Robertson, R (on the application of) v Wakefield Metropolitan Council* [2001] EWHC 915 (Admin).
20 ICO website: https://ico.org.uk/for-organisations/guide-to-data-protection/.
21 See Chapter XII.
22 The ICO maintains information concerning adequacy decisions, including details of countries that have been evaluated as providing adequate protection, at https://ico.org.uk/for-organisations/dp-at-the-end-of-the-transition-period/data-protection-now-the-transition-period-has-ended/the-gdpr/international-data-transfers/.
23 Articles 13 and 14 of the GDPR.
24 ICO website: https://ico.org.uk/for-organisations/guide-to-data-protection/guide-to-the-general-data-protection-regulation-gdpr/the-right-to-be-informed/what-privacy-information-should-we-provide/.
25 Department for Education website: www.gov.uk/government/publications/data-protection-toolkit-for-schools.
26 Paragraphs 6 to 28.
27 See Chapter XII.
28 Section 9 of the Data Protection Act 2018.
29 ICO website: https://ico.org.uk/for-organisations/guide-to-data-protection/guide-to-the-general-data-protection-regulation-gdpr/children-and-the-gdpr/how-does-the-right-to-be-informed-apply-to-children/.
30 Section 123 of the Data Protection Act 2018 uses the term 'likely', which presents some not inconsiderable difficulty in appreciating the provision's full intended scope.
31 Section 123 of the Data Protection Act 2018.
32 ICO website: https://ico.org.uk/for-organisations/guide-to-data-protection/guide-to-the-general-data-protection-regulation-gdpr/accountability-and-governance/data-protection-by-design-and-default/.
33 Explained in Chapter XII.
34 ICO website: https://ico.org.uk/for-organisations/accountability-framework/.
35 ICO website: https://ico.org.uk/media/action-weve-taken/mpns/2616742/doorstop-mpn-20191217.pdf.
36 Annex 5 to the Article 29 Working Party Publication: "Guidelines for Data Protection Officers (DPOs)", 16/ENWP 243rev.01, as formally adopted by the European Data Protection Board on its establishment.
37 European Commission website: https://ec.europa.eu/information_society/newsroom/image/document/2016-51/wp243_en_40855.pdf.

38 Article 35(7) of the GDPR.
39 [2017] EWCA Cov 74.
40 Section 53 of the Data Protection Act 2018.
41 ICO website: https://ico.org.uk/for-organisations/data-protection-advice-for-small-organisations/frequently-asked-questions/right-of-accesssubject-access-requests-and-other-rights/#whencan; see "On what grounds can a subject access request be refused entirely?".
42 Schedules 2 to 4 of the Data Protection Act 2018.
43 Information Commissioner's Annual Report and Accounts 2019/2020.
44 Schedule 12(2)(4) of the Data Protection Act 2018.
45 ICO website: https://ico.org.uk/media/about-the-ico/documents/2259467/regulatory-action-policy.pdf.
46 Section 142(1)(a) of the Data Protection Act 2018.
47 See note 45 above.
48 Taken from the statutory instruments amending the EU GDPR so it becomes the UK GDPR (see note 5 above). It can be expected that there will be conversion to sterling for post-Brexit purposes.
49 ICO website: https://ico.org.uk/action-weve-taken/enforcement/leo-kirk/.
50 ICO website: https://ico.org.uk/for-organisations/guide-to-data-protection/guide-to-the-general-data-protection-regulation-gdpr/codes-of-conduct-detailed-guidance/how-do-we-develop-a-code-of-conduct/.
51 ICO website: https://ico.org.uk/media/for-organisations/documents/2013559/big-data-ai-ml-and-data-protection.pdf.
52 Recital 71 of the EU GDPR.
53 Article 22(3) of the GDPR.
54 ICO website: https://ico.org.uk/for-organisations/guide-to-data-protection/key-data-protection-themes/guidance-on-ai-and-data-protection/what-are-the-accountability-and-governance-implications-of-ai/.
55 ICO website: https://ico.org.uk/for-organisations/guide-to-data-protection/key-data-protection-themes/explaining-decisions-made-with-ai/.
56 See reference sources for Chapter XIII for details.
57 See reference sources for Chapter XIII for details.
58 *WM Morrison (Supermarkets) Limited (Appellant) v Various Claimants (Respondents)* [2020] UKSC12.
59 Reported in *Tech Crunch*, 16 October 2020: https://techcrunch.com/2020/10/16/iab-europes-ad-tracking-consent-framework-found-to-fail-gdpr-standard/?guccounter=1&guce_referrer=aHRocHM6Ly93d3cuZ29vZ2xlLmNvbS8&guce_referrer_sig=AQAAAHQSlyAPpezuMxoUC4WSPmFtQXXBp6toURpGcYgoKIBl-AHPCVfRwok_a4nef3OfGrged79R4cKc5GKht5abTPSuXacYwGIsr2USeYoSIFKARPEDKarZu92CQWAzcY6_BuMMGupuZWrxJckTGUQK6US7aeSNs1BpXIlSLrSiH6SA.
60 ICO website: https://ico.org.uk/media/about-the-ico/documents/2615156/adtech-real-time-bidding-report-201906.pdf.
61 *Ibid.*
62 *R (On the Application of Edward Bridges) v The Chief Constable of South Wales Police* [2020] EWCA Civil 1058.
63 ICO website: https://ico.org.uk/about-the-ico/news-and-events/ai-blog-human-bias-and-discrimination-in-ai-systems/.

Reference sources

Chapter I

"An overview of the Data Protection Act 2018", ICO website: https://ico.org.uk/media/for-organisations/documents/2614158 /ico-introduction-to-the-data-protection-bill.pdf.

Chapter IV

The ICO provides an extensive guide to the lawful obtaining of consent in this section of its website: https://ico.org.uk/for-organisations/guide-to-data-protection/guide-to-the-general-data-protection-regulation-gdpr/consent/.

For a guide to the use of the legitimate interests basis for data processing, see: https://ico.org.uk/for-organisations/guide-to-data-protection/guide-to-the-general-data-protection-regulation-gdpr /legitimate-interests/.

Chapter VIII

The ICO has established a Children's Code hub within its website providing access to the Age Appropriate Design Code and related materials: https://ico.org.uk/for-organisations/childrens-code-hub/.

The full text of the Age Appropriate Design Code of Practice can be found here: https://ico.org.uk/for-organisations/guide-to-data-protection/key-data-protection-themes/age-appropriate-design-a-code-of-practice-for-online-services/.

Chapter IX

"In the Picture: A data protection code of protection for surveillance cameras and personal information", ICO website: https://ico.org.uk/media/for-organisations/documents/1542 /cctv-code-of-practice.pdf.

Chapter X

ICO Accountability Framework, ICO website: https://ico.org.uk /for-organisations/accountability-framework/.

ICO Guidance Data Protection Impact Assessments, ICO website: https://ico.org.uk/for-organisations/guide-to-data-protection /guide-to-the-general-data-protection-regulation-gdpr/ accountability-and-governance/data-protection-impact-assessments/.

Chapter XI

ICO Guide to Data Subject Access Rights, ICO website: https://ico.org.uk/for-organisations/guide-to-data-protection/guide-to-the-general-data-protection-regulation-gdpr/right-of-access/.

Chapter XII

ICO Regulatory Action Policy, ICO website: https://ico.org.uk/media/about-the-ico/documents/2259467/regulatory-action-policy.pdf.

ICO Prosecution Policy, ICO website: https://ico.org.uk/media/about-the-ico/policies-and-procedures/1882/ico-prosecution-policy-statement.pdf.

Chapter XIII

"Big data, artificial intelligence, machine learning and data protection", second edition, ICO website: https://ico.org.uk/media/for-organisations/documents/2013559/big-data-ai-ml-and-data-protection.pdf.

Explaining decisions made with AI: ICO and the Alan Turing Institute, ICO website: https://ico.org.uk/for-organisations/guide-to-data-protection/key-data-protection-themes/explaining-decisions-made-with-ai/.

ICO Auditing Framework for Artificial Intelligence: ICO website, https://ico.org.uk/about-the-ico/news-and-events/ai-auditing-framework/.

Chapter XIV

South Wales Police: Press Release – the Court of Appeal decision, www.south-wales.police.uk/en/newsroom/response-to-the-court-of-appeal-judgment-on-the-use-of-facial-recognition-technology/.

"Human bias and discrimination in AI systems" blog, ICO website: https://ico.org.uk/about-the-ico/news-and-events/ai-blog-human-bias-and-discrimination-in-ai-systems/.

About the author

Frank Suttie
Director, commercial law, Freeths LLP
frank.suttie@freeths.co.uk

Frank Suttie is a commercial law practitioner with UK law firm Freeths. A graduate in both accountancy and law, Frank advises both public and private sector clients on data protection and privacy matters.

He is particularly recognised for his work in the education sector having played a leading role in the development of data protection compliance programmes across a number of colleges, schools and academy trusts and more recently becoming an adviser to a number of education technology businesses.

About Globe Law and Business

Globe Law and Business was established in 2005. From the very beginning, we set out to create law books which are sufficiently high level to be of real use to the experienced professional, yet still accessible and easy to navigate. Most of our authors are drawn from Magic Circle and other top commercial firms, both in the UK and internationally.

Our titles are carefully produced, with the utmost attention paid to editorial, design and production processes. We hope this results in high-quality publications that are easy to read, and a pleasure to own. Our titles are also available as ebooks, which are compatible with most desktop, laptop and tablet devices. In 2018 we expanded our portfolio to include journals and Special Reports, available both digitally and in hard copy format, and produced to the same high standards as our books.

We'd very much like to hear from you with your thoughts and ideas for improving what we offer. Please do feel free to email me at sian@globelawandbusiness.com with your views.

Sian O'Neill
Managing director
Globe Law and Business
www.globelawandbusiness.com

www.ingramcontent.com/pod-product-compliance
Ingram Content Group UK Ltd.
Pitfield, Milton Keynes, MK11 3LW, UK
UKHW050258170926
8657IPUK00016B/169